Old Friends: Bill Gaither and Jake Hess share a love of gospel music.

Foreword

To understand Jake Hess, you first have to understand the word "spirit." You are not around him very long before you realize that this man is bigger than life. There is an indestructible "spirit" about him that looks into the face of all odds and shouts a resounding "yes," in spite of unbelievable circumstances. People, young and old alike, love to be around Jake because of his contagious spirit. There is a graciousness about him that genuinely "rejoices when a brother rejoices and sincerely weeps when a brother weeps."

No wonder he is one of the most loved people in the gospel music field today—a wonderful role model for aspiring young artists.

For the first time, this book will give the many friends of Jake a chance to know what many of us knew all along—a man who has been at the top, yet has kept his family priorities straight.

Even through extremely difficult health problems, he has never lost his optimistic spirit about life. He still smiles through his tears.

I thank God every day for giving me in these past few years the opportunity of getting to know a real giant, a man who was a hero of my youth. And when I got to know him better, I found that the giant was as big as I thought he was.

Now, I'm glad that the world will know what many of us have known all along ... Jake Hess is bigger than life—a spirit that I believe will live on long after he is gone.

BILL GAITHER
Alexandria, Indiana

New friends: Singer Jake Hess and writer Richard Hyatt.

A Note from the Author

My editor was on one of her non-stop trips from the mailbox to the trash can when for some reason she stopped off at my desk. While we talked, she sorted through that day's stack of mail and something in one of the envelopes caught her eye. She gave it a second glance, then she threw it in the general direction of my cluttered desk.

"You ever hear of this guy?" she asked.

It was a one-page news release from someone named Nancy Dunne. She was telling us that Jake Hess had retired from gospel music and had moved to Columbus, Georgia.

Yes, I had heard of Jake Hess.

So had a little boy who grew up in Atlanta. Every Friday or Saturday and sometimes both, his parents would put him in the car and take off. They went where the quartets went—the Atlanta City Auditorium for All-Night Singings, East Point, Columbus, Rome, Macon and numerous crossroads in between.

That little boy knew Jake Hess. He also knew Hovie, Chief, Doy, Bervin, Bobby, Denver, Cat, Rosie and the others who were The Statesmen Quartet. He heard them on the radio, sponsored by Adams Motors, where Hovie promised cars were "cleaner than a hound's tooth." He stood in line to buy their photographs, though the piano bench was already overflowing. He bought their 78s, though he broke them one by one.

The Statesmen were on WCON and the radio station wasn't far from the bus stop in Atlanta where the little boy and his mother got off to go to Rich's Department Store. His mother knew he would enjoy watching them sing so they started going to the studio. Then, when Hovie Lister did his shift as a DJ, the boy would go into the tiny booth and sit on his knee.

Yes, he knew Jake Hess.

At one of the sunup to sundown singings at the old auditorium in Atlanta, the family snapped the boy's photograph with Jake. That snapshot became a treasure that ranked right up there with his collection of Atlanta Cracker autographs.

His folks had a radio console with a record player that swung out and played a stack of 78s and the little boy would put on those blue-labeled Capitol records. Standing in front of a mirror, using a broom handle for his microphone, when The Statesmen sang, he sang. He knew every word. He knew every part. He could sing as low as Chief or as high as Denver. He could make his eyes as big as Jake's. He could pound that piano like Hovie.

Along the way, he discovered things other than gospel music. He went his way and The Statesmen went theirs.

Finally, the boy became a man and the man became a newspaper reporter.

He was at a reception in Atlanta honoring inductees into the Georgia Music Hall of Fame, a list that included Hovie Lister. He remembered Hovie, even if Hovie didn't remember that little boy who helped him spin records.

One Sunday in Columbus, he noticed an ad that said The Masters V were going to sing that afternoon at a local church. He had read about how those legends had joined together, how they were singing the old songs. He decided to go. He went early, visited with Hovie and Jake and bought one of their song books so that when he and his wife were traveling they would have the words to the songs they sang to pass the time.

In the back of his newspaper mind, he sketched out a magazine article on gospel music. He collected the notes he assembled talking with Hovie and Jake. He saved the ones he had taken years before when he had lunch with The Oak Ridge Boys. Someday, he would put that piece together.

So now the editor was asking if he had heard of Jake Hess.

Sure, he said, and he wanted to do a story on him. They planned it for an upcoming Sunday and the reporter made an appointment with Jake, who was living next to a picturesque little pond on the outskirts of Columbus.

That little boy back in Atlanta would have enjoyed that morning for the newsman asked questions the boy would have wanted him to ask. Along the way, the interview ended and the visit began. This legend turned out to be a man he could like. Even if he wasn't a little boy anymore and even if he was bald as Middle C.

He mentioned that to Jake.

"We've gone full circle. I remember when I had a head full of hair and when you didn't have much and I remember when all of a sudden you had lots of it. Now we're sitting here and I don't have any and your head is full of hair."

Jake laughed out loud. "I have lots of it in the other room," he said, "Want to borrow some?"

Since that morning they have become close enough for Jake to trust him with the story he has never told in full. Because of Jake, the reporter has had conversations with scores of gospel music people.

He has been in the studio when Bill Gaither was recording videos. He has been backstage while Jake sang on The Grand Old Opry. He has sat in Jake's den and listened to an endless assortment of memories. He has gone through boxes filled with photographs and keepsakes.

All of the conversations were recorded. It was the reporter's job to listen and transcribe. He has marveled at how many people said Jake Hess was their best friend. He listened to them freely share their feelings about a man who was more than a colleague.

Then he listened to Jake, starting at the beginning in the cotton fields of Haleyville, Alabama where his audience was the backside of a mule. He has heard him laugh and he has heard him cry, for this is a man who can do both and never apologize.

Now, beginning with the memories of that little boy in Atlanta who always stayed awake long enough to hear The Statesmen, this has become a book.

It is not just a book about Jake Hess, though surely it records his 67 years. It is also a book about all of us who have enjoyed his music, all of us who grew up in the South taking for granted the songs we knew and the people who sang them.

Critics write about Southern literature. Cookbooks list Southern recipes. Hollywood tries to emulate the Southern accent. Academicians draw the imaginary boundaries of the Bible Belt. Football fans fight over their favorite college team. These things and more are part of us and so is gospel music.

We know the lyrics. We may not remember what we had for lunch yesterday, but if somebody sits down at the piano and starts playing one of those old songs, we sing along and we never miss a word. The faith in those songs was good for our fathers and it's good enough for us. It is part of what makes us who we are. It is part of our Southern fabric, just like those scraps of cloth our grandmothers pieced together in a quilt.

As that reporter has gotten to know Jake Hess, he has also become reacquainted with the little boy he left behind. He has realized that parts of that legacy are being passed down to Kaitlin, his little girl, who is about the same age her father was when he sang into that broomstick.

Kaitlin gets up and dances when a Bill Gaither video is playing on the VCR and a quartet gets lively. And when he told Jake that she had made her debut singing "Jesus Loves the Little Children" as an intro to a teenaged choir's rendition of "Everything Is Beautiful," Jake just laughed. He didn't remind the reporter that back at his house was a Grammy Award for that very song.

These ingredients have helped make this a book. It is a book that the reporter had been preparing to write longer than he can remember. It is one he was meant to write. His prayer is that it does justice to the man whose story it tells.

Yes, I have heard of Jake Hess.

And he is everything that little boy thought he would be.

RICHARD HYATT
Columbus, Georgia

1

Prayer Was the Key

Sometimes the show backstage at the Grand Ole Opry is even more entertaining than the one seen by the people with the Saturday night tickets and this was one of those evenings. Country music star Vince Gill was in the building, trailed by an entourage of followers who swarmed outside the door of his dressing room which was entered by invitation only. Porter Wagoner had picked out one of his typically outrageous jackets and was ready to flash the audience with the lining to the coat that told folks "Hi" and "Bye." Whispering Bill Anderson, a star of another generation, was on the show, sporting hair that hadn't moved since 1975. Mingling with the country music people were a number of professional golfers from the PGA's Senior Tour, putting aside their putters to pose with the pickers. There was even a John Wayne wannabe, wearing a cowboy hat the size of Rhode Island, posing for pictures with anyone who loved the Duke.

Slumped on a lonely stool at the corner of the stage, away from all of the show business commotion, Jake Hess looked very tired and very old. In a few minutes, they would be calling his name and he was expected to sing, just as he had been doing for more than 50 years of his life. Only this particular night, with a worldwide television audience watching, for the first time in his career he didn't know if he even wanted to sing.

This was a new feeling for him. Over the years, he had suffered enough illnesses to fill a medical book, but always—

More than 40 years ago, J.D. Sumner introduced buses to gospel music and he's still riding, joined on this trip by his old buddy, Jake Hess.

even if he was coming from or going to the hospital—something inside of him yearned to sing. It was more than a yearning. It was more like a command. From the first time a traveling quartet came through his hometown in North Alabama, gospel music had been his life.

All he had ever wanted was to be a Quartet Man, a lead singer. Not this night. He was tired and he was scared. He wondered if he would ever have that old desire again.

This night was important, too. Southern gospel music was going to be seen and heard in prime time. Bob Whitaker, the Opry's vice president and general manager, did not mind confessing that he was a frustrated gospel singer. Nothing gave him any more pleasure than standing around a piano and singing old gospel favorites. And, since he did the booking, Whitaker had invited Jake Hess along with J.D. Sumner and the Stamps Quartet and Gold City to perform on the Opry's coveted televised segment.

Country singers shamelessly lobby to be featured on that 30-minute portion but Whitaker had ignored them. Even Vince Gill and his portfolio of Gold Records was only going to sing for the live audience. This Saturday night, the world was going to hear some old-fashioned quartet harmony. As for Whitaker, he was going to spend the evening with two of his heroes—Jake and J.D.

A student of history would recognize that Whitaker was keeping alive a tradition. The old Ryman Auditorium, where the Opry legend began to grow in 1943, was built in 1891 by a steamship captain who intended the hall to be a tabernacle, a church.

Even after the pickers started performing there, country music shows always included a sacred song, usually sung at a reverent spot near the end of the set. Picture a Lester Flatt, his hat over his heart, singing an old hymn. Even Hank Williams wrote a song about seeing the light.

Not that the Ryman only had country music on its historic stage. For it was also there that the late Wally Fowler held his first all-night singing. WSM, the flagship radio station of the Opry, would broadcast his "sundown to sunup" gospel shows the first Friday of every month. Jake and J.D. didn't need a history lesson to remember. They were there.

Those two had shared a lot of history together. Their friendship dates back to Central Florida, to the late 1940s, when they were young and so was their music. On stage, they were usually in dueling quartets, picking at each other, playing outrageous tricks and making memories they still enjoy rehashing. Off stage, these two unlikely friends, unlikely only if you measure it by their quartet image, for these are two men as close as brothers.

J.D. Sumner still rides the bus. For him, it is a home without mortgage which is appropriate since he claims that it was he who first began customizing the buses that musicians now consider a status symbol of all they do. He keeps moving, hitting his low notes for anyone who can write a check good enough for the bank to cash.

Jake Hess has given up his seat on the bus. Not without a fight, however. Doctors had been telling him for years that he needed to stay home and get off the road. The first doctor prescribed that decades ago when he was with the Statesmen Quartet. Another one agreed when he was with the Imperials. He got that same diagnosis again when J.D. checked him into hospitals all over the country when they were traveling with the Masters V.

Finally, he listened. It was that or die.

In 1993, he and his wife Joyce sold their home in Nashville and retired to Columbus, Georgia, following their daughter, Becky Buck, their grand-daughter Emmy Shea and grandson Brent. For a man who only wanted to sing, being off the bus had proven to be a difficult transition. That, coupled with his continuing battle with heart disease and diabetes, was part of the reason Jake found himself perched on that stool in Nashville, wondering if he could sing.

Not that Sumner had helped.

Instead of Jake getting to Nashville on his own, Sumner had suggested that the Stamps give him a ride on their bus. It's hard to say no to Sumner, so just after dawn on the morning before they were supposed to be at the Opry, they rolled into Columbus.

Jake lives in a residential area that has a rolling golf course as its backyard. His baggage was waiting outside in his circular driveway when Ed Hill maneuvered the bus through the comfortable subdivision and stopped in front of Jake's house.

The Stamps were on their way to Enterprise, Alabama, for a Friday night appearance before packing up for Nashville, and the plan was for Jake mainly to be along for the ride. They would surely rehearse the numbers he would sing with them at the Opry. Not that they needed much rehearsal since these were his signature songs and the guys in the Stamps long ago learned every nuance and gesture he would use.

Mainly, they wanted to visit for these aren't just colleagues, these fellows are friends. Ed Enoch sang with Jake in the Music City Singers when he was just out of the Army. Ed Hill had done stints with the Masters V and in the revitalized Statesmen. And with Sumner directing traffic in his personal seat of honor, this wasn't a bus ride that provided a lot of rest. There would be a stream of nonstop stories, some of them true, most of them followed by laughter. There was not much time for relaxing.

When they arrived in Nashville in Saturday's wee hours, Jake had the Stamps take him to his favorite motel. His family was staying elsewhere, but he insisted on staying where he had always stayed. He liked familiar surroundings. He would be more comfortable there. Only when he arrived, there had been a mixup. Hess had to call his longtime assistant, Nancy Dunne, to straighten things out and get him into his room. So by the time Jake got to the Opry complex late that afternoon, he was feeling every day of his 66 years.

Whitaker met him in the sprawling complex that is part of the Opryland Park and filled him in on what was going to happen that night. Only then did Jake learn that they would be singing live on the Nashville Network. He had told friends that they were just going to be singing in a small hall, certainly not on the big stage.

For the Opry staff, this was just a schedule on two yellow sheets of paper, breaking it down minute by minute for what they routinely designated as show No. 949424. There would be a TV interview with Wagoner on Opry Backstage, a show they did before the main event. There was a private mirrored dressing room where the groups could rest and warm up. Whitaker said Buck White of the Whites would be the host for the gospel segment.

Family and friends milled around Jake and one look at him was enough for them to know he was in trouble. They asked the inevitable question and he gave the predictable answer.

"Are you all right?" they asked.

"Nothin' but fine," he kept repeating, giving the answer he always gave, whether they were backstage in Nashville or in the ICU of a nameless hospital. Looking at him, they knew better.

When the yellow schedule said it was time, Jake left the dressing room and commandeered the stool at the edge of the curtain. He needed to be off his feet and he knew that the 30-minute segment moves at the pace of an old radio show, stopping and starting between commercial breaks with many of the messages being delivered by announcer Keith Bilbey at a microphone across the stage from where he sat on that stool.

It was Show Time.

The Whites opened with a rousing bluegrass number, coming together with their trademark family harmonies. People in the audience who had waited for a night at the Opry for a long time left their seats and came toward the stage armed with cameras that ranged from professional models to the disposable ones. Their exploding flashbulbs made it look like there were fireflies twinkling in front of the stage. As they snapped their photographs, they turned around in an orderly manner and went back to their seats.

When he and his daughters were through with their song, Buck White told the audience what was ahead, that tonight they were in for an unusual treat, some good old gospel music. Then he gave the cue for the first commercial spot and started off stage. The words were hardly out of his mouth before the stage crew began preparing for Gold City, a popular new quartet that recaptures many of the old quartet sounds.

White remembers well what he saw when he came off stage. Until that night, he and Jake had never really met. When he lived in Texas, he used to see the Statesmen's syndicated TV show and more recently he had watched Jake on the Bill Gaither videos, usually getting a blessing and usually ending up with tears rolling down his cheeks. The Christmas before, he

Bob Whitaker, right, is vice president of the Grand Ole Opry but is also a frustrated gospel singer. He and Ron Smith, one of TNT's talented technicians joined Jake backstage in Nashville.

and his son-in-law, country music star Ricky Skaggs, had exchanged Gaither videos, planning to trade them back and forth. So White had seen enough of Jake over the years to know something wasn't right.

He walked straight to Jake.

"He looked like he needed a lift so I walked over to him and told him how much he meant to people and how loved he was. I told him he was going to be fine then I asked him if he wanted me to say a little prayer," White said.

For White to even suggest that on the Opry stage shows how times have changed from the days when the hard-charging singers used to slip out of the Ryman and sneak away for a quick drink down the alley at Tootsie's. Very few of that old crowd would have done what White did that night.

"Something just urged me to go to him. It was like I was told to. I carry a little container of anointing oil in my pocket, in case someone's hurting. I put some on Jake's fore-head and said a prayer, asking the Lord to be with him. It was a short little prayer and when I finished, Jake stood up and smiled," White said.

The prayer may have been brief, but it got results.

"When I looked at his face, I thought I had done the right thing. Everybody won't accept that and when they don't you know it's your idea instead of the Lord's. I've tried to do it before and it didn't work," he said.

That night it worked. Someone watching might have thought that his ego had made Jake Hess stand so straight when J.D. Sumner started to introduce him.

"It was the Lord," Jake says. "While Buck was praying, I could feel it start down in my toes."

Old J.D. stretched that introduction as only he can do. He sounded like he was going to lapse into one of his trademark record spiels, but this time he was selling perhaps his oldest friend.

Tim Riley had been standing off to the side, just watch-ing. He's the bass singer for Gold City but this night he was also a fan. He had greeted Jake earlier and he was worried about him. When his group left the stage, he went into the wings to watch Jake sing with the Stamps. He marveled at the transformation.

"It was like he got a dose of feel-good," Riley said. "He got this big smile on his face and when J.D. called his name I knew he was ready."

"He's Mister Lead Singer," J.D. said, bringing Jake onto the hardwood floor of the Opry stage.

Moments before, Jake didn't know if he wanted to sing, much less whether he was able. Now he was under the lights with that ageless stage set that looks like an old red barn behind him. The Stamps also were behind him. So was J.D., cupping a hand over his ear like he always did so he could hear his notes.

He was at home, and how appropriate was the song they began to sing. Jake Hess had sung it many, many times over the years ever since he introduced it with the Statesmen in 1957. That particular night, "Prayer Is The Key To Heaven But Faith Unlocks The Door" took on a special meaning.

In the crowd, people began to recognize this lanky man in the blue suit, the way he twisted the words, the way he put his hands to work, the way his eyes seemed to explode, the way he delivered a message as well as a lyric.

It was Jake Hess, all right.

They felt they knew him, and really they did, for over the years they had shared a lot of moments together. And there he was, still singing. They cheered for Jake and they cheered for J.D. when he did the recitation that had been the trademark of Jim Wetherington, the man everyone called the Chief.

Moments before, Jake didn't know if he even wanted to sing, but after Buck White's prayer, he thrilled the Opry audience with several old favorites, joined by the Stamps Quartet and Gold City.

Almost a year to the day before Bob Whitaker put together his Prime Time Gospel, Jake Hess had announced his retirement from gospel music and without fanfare moved to Georgia.

When he first got there in early June of 1993, while contractors were building their new home, he and Joyce lived in a house by a peaceful lake near Columbus. The bus didn't load up for weekend dates and the telephone didn't ring as often as it had. There were times when Jake wondered if people remembered him or the music he had helped make so much a part of people's lives.

Except for singing for Bill Gaither's cameras in the privacy of a studio, he had done very little singing since that time. He couldn't have if he wanted to. He had decided he was only good for a couple of songs. The years had taken away his endurance. But now he was back, singing with friends and for friends.

By the time they did their finale, all of the groups were on stage together. At every microphone there were two voices. Jake Hess stood alone in the middle. Watching all of this unfold, Bob Whitaker couldn't stand it. Remembering when he was a young man singing with his brothers and how like other would-be singers he had imitated the Jake Hess style. The Grand Ole Opry executive bounded on to the stage and shared a mike with his hero. At that moment, you could have sold Whitaker a ticket for he was having as much fun as the people in the cheap seats.

There was music and there was emotion, and that night in Nashville people reminded Jake Hess that they definitely remembered. Applause rippled throughout the packed auditorium. There were standing ovations and there were tears. Not only for the past but for the present.

It truly was nothin' but fine.

Jake, right, was 9 years old when he and his brother Chris went to a family reunion. That meant the clothes they were wearing were their Sunday best.

2

Singing to an Alabama Mule

They called their new baby W.J. It is easy to run out of names by the time the 12th of 12 children arrives and that may be what happened to Stovall and Lydia Hess. They had 11 children ranging in age from 2 to 24 when the seventh son was born on Christmas Eve in 1927. So he became just plain W.J., or so he thought for the next 52 years of his life.

A quartet singing legend named John Daniel had christened him Jake Hess along the way, but the draft board in Lancaster County, Nebraska, decided otherwise. He was living in Lincoln when it came time to register with Uncle Sam. Sitting down at a desk, they began asking questions, starting

Sharecroppers, William Stovall and Lydia Hess had 12 children that they reared on North Alabama farms.

with the most simple one.

"Name?"

"W.J. Hess."

"No, your full name."

"That's it. W.J. Hess."

When he persisted, the woman stormed away and went to get her supervisor.

"Young man, we do not have time to play games. This is serious. Now please give us your full name." the supervisor insisted.

When he insisted that W.J. Hess was the name his folks

had given him back in Haleyville, Alabama, she told him that wouldn't do, that he was required to have a name—not just initials—and that W.J. Hess would not qualify for the United States government.

"Has there been anyone in your family named William?"

"Well, my pop's name is William Stovall Hess."

"OK, your first name is William."

"Do you have any relatives with a name that begins with the letter 'J'?"

"I have an Uncle Jesse," he said.

"That's it. You are named William Jesse Hess," she said.

His singing buddies had been calling him Wonly Jonly— as in W-only, J-only. Now he had an official name. Or so he thought until many years later when he applied for a passport. You had to have a birth certificate to get one so he called the proper office in Montgomery, Alabama, the state capital. He had sent all the information but nothing came in the mail so he called to see what the problem was.

"Mr. Hess, you don't have a name," the woman in the state office said.

"Yes, mam, I do. It is W.J. Hess. I was born in a community they called Mt. Pisgah in Limestone County, Alabama, on December 24, 1927. I think it was a Doctor Maples who delivered me," he said.

"We have all of that and I know who you are. I've heard of you. I've heard you sing," she said. "But you do not have a name. All the records show is that on that particular date, there was a 'Man Child' born to Stovall and Lydia Hess."

For the next two weeks, as far as the State of Alabama bureaucracy was concerned, he was known as "Man Child Hess." But finally she called him back to say they had been able to work things out.

"So, what do you want your name to be?" she said.

He didn't know what to say.

"Think about it. Who do you want to be? You can be anybody you want to be."

"I've been paying Social Security all these years on W. Jake Hess," he said.

"OK," she said. "From now on, that is your name."

Most of his life, the world has known him simply as Jake Hess, a Quartet Man in a well-pressed suit, who has stood in a spotlight singing gospel music. He has accumulated awards and rewards and has sung his songs around the world.

But the W.J. Hess who was born in the isolated hills of North Alabama was as far away from that kind of life as the notes at either end of an octave.

The Hess family was sharecroppers. They depended on

Growing up, Jake Hess used to sing to the backside of a mule as he plowed, hoping that one day he would leave the farm and become a Quartet Man.

the overworked land for their lives and the land they tilled belonged to someone else. They grew cotton and corn, just like their neighbors did. They were at the mercy of the weather, the boll weevil and the people who set the prices on their crops. The land they planted was as tired and drained as the people who farmed it. This was before anyone knew anything about rotating crops or taking care of the soil and even if they did, there was no time for anything foolish like that. There was only time to work.

Stovall and Lydia had given birth to Birdie, Clement, Othie, Ollie, Arnell, Gerthie, Varnell, Cleveland, Eudora, Izora, Chrystel and, finally, W.J. By the time their last child came along, Birdie and Arnell, two of their older children, were already dead. But there still was enough of them to work a farm and work they did, from the time they could walk and handle a hoe. There was enough of them to "lay by" their own fields in time for the family, kids and all, to hire out to their neighbors.

Large families came in handy, for the farm machinery they used was the kind that breathed and bled. There were no tractors. Stovall Hess didn't even own a mule to pull the plow. The landowner did, but he didn't. He could depend only on the Lord and his family.

"I first remember going to the field to pick and plow," Jake Hess says. "I knew that some way, some place, there was a better life. I didn't mind the work. I just didn't want to farm. All I ever wanted to do was sing."

There did not seem to be much to sing about in those dreary years. Two years after he was born, history books report that the Great Depression began. For the people who lived where he did, 1929 was just another year. Wall Street didn't matter to them. Only the road that ran in front of the house where they lived.

Hemmed in by the hills and with only a network of dirt roads going in and out, this area of the country was an untouched universe. Industrialization wouldn't get there for years. This was a generation before Roosevelt and the TVA turned on the lights.

People sincerely believed they were locked to the land on which they were born. That was their world. They thought there was no escape, and in many ways, there wasn't. If your daddy was a farmer, then you were a farmer. Dreams meant nothing. Only the soil was important.

The Hess family moved all over that part of Alabama, looking for richer soil and a better place to live. It was a hard life and if you weren't careful, it could harden you.

"We were poor," Jake says. "Even the poor people knew we were poor."

Their salvation was music. They had an old pump organ that moved when they moved. But most of their music was made when the family gathered around to sing, using those softback song books put out twice a year by James D. Vaughan, whose publishing company was just up the road in Lawrenceberg, Tennessee.

When W.J. was a baby, his brothers took him with them to see Vaughan who even then was a legend.

"I sat on Brother James' knee and pulled on those funny stickup collars he wore. I thought they were the silliest things I had ever seen and they probably were. I remember that he was a Godly man who would talk to us about the Lord. It thrilled us to death," he says.

Vaughan had been born in the waning days of the Civil War. He was a devout member of the Church of the Nazarene, a holiness denomination that loved music that sang about the love of God. This music gave a different voice and a different

The John Daniel Quartet was a dominant group in the 1940s. They not only sang, they sold, from songbooks to socks. Standing around the piano are John Daniel, Jake, Troy Daniel, Ottis Williams and Lonnie Williams. Everett Buttram was the pianist.

message than the more formal Broadman Hymnals used by the Baptists or the Cokesbury books that were popular with the Methodists. It was evangelical and it was happy with simple lyrics that plain folks could understand.

This was the kind of music Vaughan and his disciples taught in his schools, teaching his first class in 1883 and forming his first quartet about that time. Like the ones that followed, it was four men and a piano.

During the 1920s, Vaughan became the father of Southern gospel music, putting business in harmony with the message. He put his quartets on his own radio station. He recorded the first gospel records. He put groups on the road—the first one was in 1910—to sing the songs and, yes, to sell the songbooks he was publishing two times a year.

Along with Stamps-Baxter, his primary competitor, they supported groups all over the country, even buying automobiles so they could not only get themselves to their concert dates but the songbooks they were hauling in the trunk of that car. Both of them demanded loyalty. If you were a Vaughan group, you sang Vaughan songs. Anyone caught singing a Stamps-Baxter number was in trouble.

Stovall Hess loved this music and he saw to it that his children learned about it. They were taught shaped notes, a form of musical notation that began in New England before spreading South to the singing schools. Every shape had a sound and every note had a shape. *Do* was the house top. *Re* was like a wash pot. *Mi* was the diamond. *Fa* was a rectangle. *Sol* was the circle. *La* was the square. *Te* was the ice cream cone. And then it was back to *Do*.

"I don't even remember when I first learned the shaped notes. I don't even know how I learned. I guess Pop or my brothers taught me," Jake says.

Stovall Hess had written a few songs for two nearby publishing companies and he and his older sons all taught in singing schools. Such schools were more than places to learn about the Bible or about music. They were also social events. They were places you got caught up on the latest news. There was no television and only a few folks had radios. Nobody had the money for a movie even if there had been a theater there. But they had their faith and they had their music. They sang about the promise of a Better Place, a place where the streets were paved with gold instead of clay and where the family circle would be unbroken.

There was a singing just about every Sunday somewhere in the area and people came to expect the Hess family to be there. The singings started early in the morning and continued throughout the day, breaking only for a potluck lunch served outside on the church grounds. Even if you couldn't sing very well, you could wring a hen's neck and cook up a pot of peas and feed the folks who did.

Usually, somebody would ask the Hess brothers to do a few songs. The older boys would oblige and along the way, they started including little W.J., who had been tugging at his brothers' pants legs begging them to let him sing a song. Soon, he became either a novelty or a star. Folks thought it was cute to see this little fellow who had to stand on a box so he could be seen.

The first solo Jake performed was "Harmonies of Heaven" doing it in a clear tenor voice that everyone bragged on, tousling the hair on his head, telling him that one day he would sing in a quartet just like his brothers.

"You can get by with a lot when you're 5 years old," he laughs.

Not that he could get away with anything at home. Even though he was the baby of the brood, his folks expected him to follow their instructions. His mother had a way of keeping him in line.

"She would tell me the boogey man was going to get me. Then she started saying there was something behind that big bush out there and it was gonna get me. It usually worked," he remembers.

Until this one night.

He heard that threat long enough.

"I had heard that so long that it bugged me. I was scared to death but I started crying as loud as I could. I went out there and parted that bush and nothing was there. It broke my heart. My mama had told me a story and if you can't believe your mama, who can you believe?"

But you better believe that the Hess boys worked. However, even then, out there in the sun, he couldn't get that music out of his head.

"Plowing the field from one end to the other, I would sing to the backside of that mule. I just knew that someday I would get to sing with a quartet instead of that old mule," he says.

As he got older, there were places other than the fields to sing. He started helping in the singing schools with his father and brothers, even joining them for a long trip to a school in Missouri. Most of the time, he would teach the rudiments of music, but they were late getting there and someone else was already teaching that class so W.J. was asked to teach guitar.

"I didn't know the first thing about teaching guitar. The people in the class would ask a question about something and I would say they'd have to wait, that what they were asking about happened to be tomorrow's lesson. The question would be something like, 'How do you make a G-Chord.' That night, back in my room, I would find the answer and tell them the next day. And you've never heard of a hot guitarist coming out of Sikeston, Missouri, have you?"

Around Alabama, the Hess brothers were getting to be a popular group. Since their Baptist church was on a traveling circuit, services were held only twice a month so there was plenty of time on Sundays for them to sing. This only made W.J.'s dream of being a Quartet Man grow stronger. He had to be ready when the chance came, so he enrolled in a Stamps-

Those horns on top of this car would announce the arrival of The Daniel Quartet. Jake enjoyed this duty because he could hear his voice bouncing around the town. Troy Daniel and Jud Phillips assembled this lineup after a falling-out with Troy's brother John over the name of the original group.

Baxter normal school to study harmony. It was being conducted by W. Lee Higgins, a prominent teacher and singer.

After the school was over, Higgins, who knew the young man's strong desire to sing, took him aside and offered some stinging advice.

"Young man, if you study, you can become a great music instructor. I know you want to be a singer, but I have to tell you, there is something about your voice that is not pleasing to the ear," said Higgins, who decades later would buy tickets to hear that unpleasant voice sing.

That didn't stop his dream, however.

He would listen on the radio to a singer named Ernest Braswell, who sang lead with the Deep South Quartet out of Birmingham. He never knew too much about Braswell for Braswell never ventured too far from home, but he knew that he liked his distinctive style, his enthusiasm and the way he put special emphasis on certain words. Braswell became a major influence on W.J. Like him, the boy also wanted to sing lead, even though quartets of the time emphasized the tenor and the bass.

His father knew that the boy wanted to learn so he shared with him his own ideas about singing. Stovall Hess had never had formal music training, but the education he gave his youngest son has stuck with him ever since.

"Pop said that singing was talking on key, that the most important thing in a gospel song was the words. He told me I was going to be singing to people who needed to understand that message and that if I ever had a choice of missing a tone or a word, to miss the tone. The audience has to know what you're saying," he remembers.

Soon, W.J. Hess not only was singing with his brothers but was singing in organized groups around North Alabama. His first group was Louie Auten and the Tennessee Valley Boys.

Not long after that his brother Chris went into the Marines Corps and for a while he took his place with Lloyd George and the Rhythm Rascals. Lloyd tagged the teenager "Curly," which at the time was appropriate. The Rascals didn't sing gospel music and they would be the only group he ever sang with that didn't.

Then came an offer to sing with Ottis Williams and the Haleyville Melody Boys which was the hottest group around that part of Alabama. Their name was also popular because across the country there seemed to be a Melody Boys in every town. Williams' quartet had a radio show on WLAY in Sheffield, Alabama. That impressed a youngster who had sung with a microphone only once before in his life, when his brothers let him do a number on their show in Decatur, Alabama.

He was doing what he always wanted to do, what he felt he was called to do, but he was also working at a grocery store before and after school and at the Dr. Pepper plant at evenings. You could have dreams, but you also had to take care of reality and reality meant hard work.

While the Melody Boys were big in Haleyville, the John Daniel Quartet had a following that stretched across the entire Southeast. John Daniel was a gospel pioneer. In the 1930s and 1940s, he managed groups that over the years included singers such as Big Jim Waits, Wally Fowler and Gordon Stoker. Daniel had represented both Vaughan and Stamps-Baxter and his group was regularly featured on WSM in Nashville, the flagship station for the Grand Ole Opry. They had even sung to a national audience on NBC Radio. Ottis Williams told Daniel about this young tenor singer he had found back in Haleyville.

When John Daniel talked to W.J. Hess about singing with his quartet, that dream of getting out from behind that mule was beginning to become a reality.

Was he ready? He was barely 16 years old. He could finish high school by mail. People said he could sing, but this was the John Daniel Quartet and to him he didn't think he sang as well as his brothers Ollie, Butch, Cleveland or Chris.

But soon, there he was—with God's help, he knew— singing with the fellows he had listened to so often. He was fitted for a new suit in Birmingham which for a boy who had grown up in patched overalls was a big event. They explained to him that looking like a quartet was the first step in sounding like a good quartet. That would be a lesson he would carry with him.

Lydia Hess reared 12 children as the wife of a sharecropper who every few years moved to a new farm, hoping that crop would be a good one.

He was eager. When John Daniel was out, he sang tenor. If Troy Daniel was taking a rest, he sang lead. From time to time, he even sang baritone. He only wanted to sing.

People who came to hear them sing heard more than gospel. They would do five or six gospel tunes then go into a concert set. Taking a cue from Vaughan and Stamps-Baxter, John Daniel had a book of concert songs for sale.

Troy Daniel and Carl Raines were the group's funny men and they seldom left an audience that wasn't entertained. They were showmen, but they could also sing and their specialty was gospel. Most nights. they left the stage singing, "I Found a Hiding Place", a song John Daniel once sang for 12 minutes on the Prince Albert portion of the Grand Ole Opry.

Six of them traveled together since Daniel always had an extra man who could sing when he was conducting business. The group traveled in two cars with W.J. Hess, as the newest man, sitting in the middle. The other car had a large speaker horn mounted on the top. That car went ahead of the other one so they could drive through town announcing that the John

Daniel Quartet was coming. :"Yes, friends. Tonight is the night to see, hear and enjoy the famous John Daniel Quartet." John Daniel did not miss a trick. He was capable of selling as well as singing and they did both.

At the concerts, they sold costume jewelry, song books and records. The group got a commission of the sales, splitting 50 percent, with the other half going to Daniel who paid for the hotels, the car expenses and furnished the suits. They were always moving for the group was under contract with the Martin Theater chain so they would go into a town and sing 20-minute stands between the feature films. It was a demanding life, but W.J. Hess was enjoying every day of it.

Only John Daniel was having troubles.

Every night, he had to introduce the fellows in the group and it was confusing. There was a W.J. Hess, there was a J.W. Phillips. One night, after getting mixed up again, Daniel called a meeting.

J.W. Phillips became Jud Phillips.

W.J. Hess became Jake Hess.

And Jake Hess was fitting in well with the music. It was the life he thought it would be. Other things were bothering him though, things they didn't teach you in singing school.

From the beginning, he was uncomfortable with the selling, especially John Daniel's kind of selling. They always had something to push. Even socks. They advertised socks on the radio. But it was the costume jewelry that eventually caused a rift between the young singer and his boss.

Every night. Every town. It was the same. They would be ending the first part of their program and John Daniel would reach into his coat pocket and, to his nightly surprise, there was a pair of earrings or a necklace.

"Where did this come from?" he would say, a look of shock pasted on his face. "I sure can't carry this home. My wife would be all over me. I'll tell you what we're gonna do. Troy, get me some tickets. We'll just raffle this nice jewelry off. Ten cents a chance. Oh, make it 12 for a dollar, Troy."

The music would stop and the fellows would go to the edge of the stage and sell chances. Somebody might go up the aisle and take up money. By the time they were through, that piece of costume jewelry that might have been worth a dime would have brought in a roll of money. Many times those tickets brought in more money than the gate.

Next night. New jewelry. Same routine.

Until Tuscaloosa, Alabama.

"We got there and I knew several folks who were going to the university there. I told John that I was not going to sell those tickets anymore. He said if I thought I was too good to sell that I was fired," Jake says, noting that this was only the first time he would be fired by John Daniel, a man he still says was like a father to him.

Jake had been home only a few days before Troy Daniel called. He and his brother had split up and he was putting together a group of his own. Jud Phillips—whose brother Sam would later discover a singer named Elvis Presley—was going to be the manager. They wanted Jake to join them in Memphis. They called themselves the Daniel Quartet. They sang around there for awhile, but it didn't seem to be working out for any of them.

Jake went back with John Daniel for he was not only a Quartet Man but a businessman, one of the best Jake says he has ever worked for. After Jake left Troy's group, he was replaced by Cat Freeman, another product of Alabama's Sand Mountain, and the group became The Jolly Boys.

Back on the road The John Daniel Quartet went, covering the South as they had for years. Most of the groups worked close to home, for their popularity extended only as far as the tiny AM radio station on which they sang. There was also a shortage of gasoline during the war but this was something that never bothered John Daniel and his group.

"People would come up to us at concerts and give us gas rationing coupons, even sets of tires which you also weren't supposed to be able to buy. The only thing we had to be careful about was where we bought our gas because a lot of those coupons they would give us were T-Stickers, which were supposed to be for trucks. Most gas stations didn't really care what you used," he says.

They didn't stay off the road because of the war, but Christmas was an extended holiday for the quartet. People didn't have the money or the time at that time of the year. They were singing regularly, but Jake still didn't have enough money to buy gifts so he got a job at Elmer Shipman's dry cleaning shop there in Haleyville.

"During Christmas week, I came in to the shop to get a load of clothes. One of the guys around the presser, Jess Lee, said that some lady had brought Elmer a quart of white grape wine. 'You drink half of it and I'll drink half of it,' he said, 'then we'll fill it up with water.' I said I didn't drink but he said it was homemade and that it wouldn't make me drunk," Jake says.

He always enjoyed playing a trick and he couldn't stand it if somebody outdid him. So in a flash, Jake had turned up the bottle and consumed half of it. His co-worker did the same.

"I went back to work and I was throwing those clothes around in the car and delivering cleaning to people who had never stopped at Shipman's. I insisted they keep them. You'd think that I lost Elmer a whole lot of clothes. But the next week,

FORMAL RE-OPENING

Under New Management

Business & Professional Men's Club

Saturday, Nov. 9th

CHOICE FOODS   EFFICIENT SERVICE...

Grand Entertainment

Hess Brothers

Featuring

Garglin-Mann

at the

Piano

OLD AND NEW MEMBERS INVITED

For Reservations
Phone 42-191

Hours 5 to 12 p. m.

Business & Professional Men's Club

THELMA HOTEL

Leaving John Daniel once again, Jake joined his brothers in Lakeland, Florida where the Hess Brothers soon got a job at a local hotel.

Lydia and William Stovall Hess never owned a home or a car until their youngest son started to make a living in gospel music.

all of those folks brought them back. It was good for business because when they came in, they left their cleaning. That was the first and only time in my life that I was ever tight, the only time I ever drank."

By this time, World War II was coming to an end and, one by one, Stovall Hess' sons were coming home. He had a dream that four of his boys would sing together in a quartet. Two of them had moved to Lakeland, Florida and when Jake came home from the road, Pop Hess told him about that dream.

He called John Daniel and said he was quitting and soon he joined his brothers in Florida. In a short time, the Hess Brothers started doing well around Lakeland, Tampa and Orlando. They got a show on a radio station in Lakeland, sponsored by Banks Feed Store. They were singing at a hotel three nights a week. Pap Baxter of Stamps-Baxter had promised to send them a supply of song books to sell and a car so they could start to travel.

One Sunday afternoon, they were not booked but they decided to go to a Baptist church on Main Street in Lakeland where there was a singing going on. The Sunny South Quartet was going to be there and they wanted to see if this group was as good as people said.

"Runt Selph was the promoter of that show and he insisted that we sing a few songs. It went over well and even the other groups seemed impressed," Jake says.

The Sunny South Quartet had a tall, skinny bass singer named J.D. Sumner who still remembers the Hess Brothers' tenor with the thin voice.

Sumner was impressed.

"Jake was a completely different singer back then. You would not believe how beautiful his voice was. When he developed his style, it wasn't as beautiful as it was then," Sumner says.

To a man, the Hess brothers figured they were about to fulfill their father's hopes. Until breakfast the next morning, at least.

Jake and his brothers thought that was a break-through afternoon for their fledgling group and it seemed to be for Selph and some other local promoters had heard them and liked them. There was talk of a lot of new bookings.

"Ollie came down and he had his suitcase under his arm. Butch asked him what he was doing and where he was going. 'Home,' he said, 'to Haleyville.' He knew more music and harmony than the rest of us did and he was leaving. Butch said how well we were doing, but Ollie didn't say a word. And you know, Ollie's dead now and we never did know why he left us," Jake says, still wondering what happened.

With his brothers going their separate ways, Jake got his old job back with John Daniel and headed for Alabama. When he walked into the Moulton Hotel where the quartet lived, to his surprise, there was Troy Daniels. Neither knew the other was rejoining the group. Troy had vowed he would never work with Jake again after he left the group in Memphis. But as they walked into that hotel lobby, nothing was said.

With Daniel, Jake was making $40 a week which in the mid-1940s made him one of the highest paid singers in gospel music. He slipped right back into his former role and things were going so well that after a show one night John Daniel took him aside and told Jake he was giving him a raise in salary—all the way up to $45 a week.

The next morning, Jake told Troy Daniel how generous he thought his brother was.

"It's nice of him to give us that raise," Jake said.

"What raise?" Troy asked.

"I never thought I'd ever make $45 a week in my whole life."

"I didn't get no raise," said Troy.

Jake went straight to Daniel and said what an awful situation that was. "I pay everybody in the group what they are worth," John Daniel explained. That didn't help and Jake pitched such a fit that Daniel fired him.

Again.

"And I never did get a single $45 paycheck," he says. "But John Daniel was a fine man. One minute he fired me and the next minute he asked me if I needed any money."

While he had been in Florida, his brother Butch had introduced Jake to his friend, James Wetherington. They had met when Butch filled in with Wetherington's group. Like them, Wetherington was a farm boy, from a South Georgia town with the memorable name of Ty-Ty. By then, he was singing bass with the Melody Masters, a group that had become the chief rivals of the Sunny South Quartet.

Calling back to Florida, Wetherington told Jake the group needed a tenor and over the telephone, he was hired. He said he would be there in a few days.

Only there were several friends to stop off and see along the road from Alabama to Florida and by the time Jake got to Tampa, it had been more than the few days he had promised. By then, the Melody Masters had hired Calvin Newton for the job.

He was back in an area he didn't really care for and he was out of work. Not for long, however. Right up the road, there was an unlikely opening. He had returned to sing with their competitors, but in a few days Jake was singing lead with the Sunny South Quartet.

Overnight, he had gone from a secure spot with a major group to singing on a local circuit. Those weren't the only problems he encountered, however. Two of his brothers were still in Florida and they thought he should be singing with them.

With the vast difference in ages, he and his brothers had never been particularly close and had little in common. They had been called to war and he had been called to sing. This would be the final break.

The breakup of the Hess Brothers Quartet was effectively the end of any kind of deep relationship with his older brothers. Over the years, it appeared that they would come to see Jake's success in gospel music as a reminder of what they might have become.

Two of his brothers—Clement and Cleveland—became Baptist preachers but only once did they ever invite Jake and his various groups into their churches for a singing.

Most of his brothers ended up back around the farm in North Alabama. Whenever he would come home for a visit, it was uncomfortable.

"They kept telling me that I was going to starve to death out there on the road—and sometimes they were almost right," he says.

Stovall Hess knew what was happening. One evening, when his youngest son wandered out to the wood pile where his father was chopping wood, he stopped and put down his ax.

"W.J., I want to tell you something. Now don't you get upset with what your brothers are saying. If you do nothing but tote chips from one side of the road to the other, if God is in it and you do it long enough, then you'll make it."

And as long as Pop was alive, whenever they greeted one another, Jake Hess would smile and remind him that he was still toting chips.

Sometimes they sang. Sometimes they could do nothing but stand on the stage and laugh. J.D. Sumner, seated, and Jake have been close since the Hess Brothers came to hear Sumner's group sing in Lakeland, Florida. They started as friends, but nearly half a century later they are more like brothers. And they still enjoy laughing.

3

Big Things Are Coming

Not that long ago, Jake Hess had been concerned about being with a group that raffled off cheap trinkets and had boxes of socks to sell. Now he was in a place where he didn't feel at home, singing with a quartet that couldn't sell tickets. It was a long way from John Daniel, his matching suits and his national reputation. Now he was making his debut with the Sunny South Quartet in an out-of-the-way church, deep in the state of Florida, wondering where all the people were.

The town was Auburndale, Florida, a town where there were citrus trees and not much else, and you couldn't fill the pews of a church with bags of oranges.

"It was one of those crowds where you love to see a car coming down the road because you hope to heaven that it will turn in," remembers J.D. Sumner, who that night was providing the low notes for the Sunny South.

There were less than 20 people assembled, and that included the quartet. For Sumner, that called for a cigarette. He sneaked outside the church and lit one up. His new lead singer joined him.

"We got out there and Jake said, 'Which way is Haleyville?' As if he was fixing to just take off. He didn't say so, but he must have thought he had joined up with a bunch of losers," Sumner says.

They weren't losers. They were just struggling.

It hadn't been that long ago that Horace Floyd, the tenor and manager, had to put together an entirely new group. Like so many quartets, they had suffered internal problems and three of the guys had left to form another group.

James Wethington, Mosie Lister and Lee Kitchens went down the highway and started the Melody Masters along with Alvin Tootle and a lively pianist named Wally Varner. To make matters even worse, one group represented Vaughan and the other pushed Stamps-Baxter. That's why folks in the area thought it was so unusual for Jake to sign up with the Melody Masters and end up with the Sunny South.

"They were rivals, all right. I had kicked around there enough to know some of that, but I was a happy-go-lucky fellow who didn't get involved with all of that," Jake says.

When Wetherington left, Floyd had hired Sumner, who was studying to be a watchmaker and had never thought about becoming a member of a quartet. He sang bass and Roger Clark had come in on baritone with Quentin Hicks on the piano.

Even though the good people of Auburndale had been indifferent, this was not a group of losers. They had a radio

Baritone Roger Clark seated, joined the Sunny South Quartet at the same time as Jake, singing alongside bass singer, J.D. Sumner, right.

show and they had a generous sponsor, Dixie Lily Flour, that had bought them a big old DeSoto to get them to their jobs. More than anything, they had fun.

Such as a night at a cafe in Dade City where Jake stuck Sumner with a nickname that neither has ever forgotten. Even now, Jake calls him "George."

They had sung a date and on their way back to Lakeland the five of them had stopped in for a late-night meal. They grabbed a table that had two chairs on each side and a chair at each end.

The empty seat was next to Jake.

"Who's sitting here?" the waitress asked, sitting down a glass of water.

"George, he's gone to the bathroom," Jake said. "He'll be right back."

While they ate and the waitress kept coming back to check on them, they kept telling her about this fellow named George.

From that night on, Sumner has been George.

Jake and Sumner weren't yet 20 years old. They were growing up together. They sang like men, but they were still boys and they were still fond of childish pranks.

Most of their pranks were harmless, but several incidents they were involved in could have been anything but.

One was a wrestling match where each of them had a vice grip on the other's nose. Neither would give in and both of them were born stubborn. Rolling around in the backseat of the car, they almost jerked each other's noses right out of socket.

Another started over their love of pinball machines. Anytime the quartet was on the road and the car would stop, they would hurry inside the store and get into a game.

Floyd got tired of his bass and lead singers making the group wait on them so this one night he said the rest of the fellows were ready to go so the two pinballers had better get themselves into the car.

They did, and the car was speeding up the road when a dare was exchanged in the backseat. It started with the idea that if they got out, they could go back and play some more.

"If you jump out of the car, I'll be right behind you."

That was enough for Jake. Out he went.

A deal was a deal. George had no choice. He followed.

"It was a good thing we jumped into sand or else we'd have been in a lot of trouble," Jake says.

Noticing how many of the other singers had mustaches, they deduced that having one surely would make them better singers so the two of them decided the time had come for them to join the crowd. As their mustaches began to grow, they still didn't look just right.

"We had an office at the rear of a print shop and before we went to shows, we would go in there and rub printer's ink on our mustaches to make them darker," Jake says.

Mustaches were not their only problem. Since meals could be scarce, J.D. and Mary Sumner used to invite Jake over to eat with them. One evening, Jake was lamenting that he needed a haircut and didn't have the money to spend on a barber.

"I was a barber in the Army," Sumner said.

Jake listened while his buddy told him about all the haircuts he had done in the service. And since he also needed a trim, he said Jake could cut his hair in return.

"When I got through with him, his head looked like his hair had been cut with a bowl. It never has recovered either," Sumner laughs.

Being in the Sunny South Quartet was fun for Jake— thanks to his bass singer

"And I never did get to cut his hair either," Jake fires back.

Firing back would bring to mind a painful memory for Sumner. He had been playing around with fire crackers and one of them didn't go off. He picked it up and stuck it in his mouth, pretending it was a cigarette.

"For some reason, he took a draw on it. Old George didn't realize it, but the thing was lit and when it went off it blew the end of his nose off and tore a chunk out of his lip," Jake says.

They had told that story ever since and many years later, on a night in Indiana, Jake reminded Sumner about the incident. It was more than a reminder.

"There was this guy sitting right down in front of the stage, and he had a split in his lip, no teeth and a hole in his nose. I said, 'George, look at this guy on the front row. He's been smoking firecrackers.' That was another of those deals where we laughed all night."

This was the lineup of the Melody Masters that left Florida for South Carolina. Jake joined them in Tampa after leaving the Sunny South Quartet. Seated are Calvin Newton and James Wetherington. Standing are Wally Varner, Jake and Alvin Tootle.

They always have laughed a lot.

"I guess that the most fun I ever had in a group was with the Sunny South. We were up to something all the time. You have to be a little crazy to be in a quartet. You don't have to be, but it helps," Jake says.

Between their unpredictable antics, the Sunny South Quartet was making a name for itself around Lakeland as a solid gospel group, but whenever anyone would talk about the good quartets in the area, they always had to mention the Melody Masters.

This irked the guys in Sunny South who didn't know what folks saw in those fellows down the road in Tampa/St. Pete where their radio show had created a following.

It became a gospel war.

On stage, the groups tried to out-sing each other. Off stage, they tried to out-think one another. If one was booked and the other wasn't, they would try to find out where the other guys were singing.

"We'd chase them down the road if we had to," Sumner says.

And once they found out, they were not above trying to sabotage the other group's date. If you wanted to hurt a group, all you had to do was tinker with the sound system, or else accidentally pull the plug. These groups were capable of both tactics.

"If we were singing together on the same show, we would purposely be late so the Melody Masters would have to sing first. We would wait until they were on stage, then we'd make a big entrance, walking down the center aisle, waving and shaking hands, just to disrupt them," Sumner says, laughing at the childish competition.

Though he was having fun and was able to make a living singing his music, Jake still wasn't content. Something about

Florida did not agree with him. He was still young and there were always other jobs.

Even with the Melody Masters.

"We had heard how good a singing town Greenville was. We had played a date with The Rangers up in Jacksonville and Hovie Lister was on keyboards. He liked our sound and he said South Carolina would be a good spot for us," Varner says.

Their lead singer, Lee Kitchens, was a Florida native and he had no desire to pack up for the move. When that word reached Jake, he made an unorthodox move of his own.

He joined the enemy.

"I just wanted to get out of there. But I never sang a date with the Melody Masters in Florida," he says.

Greenville might have been a good town for gospel singing, but it did not put out much of a welcome mat for the new quartet in town.

From the beginning, they struggled.

Their only salvation was the friends they were making. Herman Lister met the newcomers at WFBC, the NBC station in Greenville. Lister, Joe Brown and some other folks were kind enough to feed the group between paychecks—which was often.

The group that arrived in South Carolina was Jake, Wetherington, Varner, Tootle and Calvin Newton, the tenor who months before had gotten that job back in Florida. Newton was a hot item in quartet circles at the time and not long after they moved he got a better job.

Jake remembered a tenor who had been almost a neighbor of his, coming out of Fyfe, Alabama, another in a long line of Sand Mountain singers. His name was G.C. Freeman, but because the high-pitched notes his tenor voice could create sometime sounded like a feline, he had always been called Cat.

Soon after the Melody Masters arrived in Greenville, South Carolina, Calvin Newton left the group and Cat Freeman took over on tenor. The nucleus of this group would play a big part in the future of gospel music. On the front row were Alvin Tootle and Wally Varner. In the rear were Freeman, James Wetherington and Jake Hess.

Without anyone knowing it, the nucleus of a gospel music landmark was coming together in a textile town in South Carolina. Not that anyone there seemed to notice, for even with the talent they had brought together, the Melody Masters were starving.

Literally.

"All five of us were staying in one small tiny room. There were two double beds and a rollaway. Every five weeks, you go the rollaway," Jake remembers.

While they were in Nebraska in 1948, the Melody Masters were members of the musical family at KFAB. Their song list ranged from old gospel numbers to popular songs like "Smoke, Smoke, Smoke That Cigarette" and "Sioux City Sue."

Sleeping was one thing. Eating was another. As nice as Lister and Brown had been to them, they felt bad about taking advantage of their hospitality.

"We had gone a day and a half without eating a thing. That may not sound like much and it's not if you know you're going to eat. But we didn't know. We were flat broke," Jake says.

The group shared a Buick—like the bed, one fellow owned it every five weeks. They started to the country, figuring they would find something they could eat.

"We drove up to Paris Mountain, just out of town, and we came up on a peach orchard and we knew what we had to do. We started loading up that old car with fresh peaches. We evermore ate peaches. That's all we had for the next three days," he says.

They were living one meal at a time.

"But you know, nobody said quit," Jake says, pointing out the commitment each of them had to what they were doing.

Just when they thought they were about to have to find another car load of fresh peaches, they talked themselves into a regular job at the Pantry, a local restaurant.

"We sang for our supper," Jake says.

Knowing they would have at least one meal a day took some of the pressure off of them and it wasn't long before the only real opportunity they found in Greenville came along.

Jake and Wetherington made a trip to a nearby Army base. This was just after World War II and there was plenty of entertainment money floating around that post. The Melody Masters had themselves a job. A real job.

"They paid us a thousand dollars," Jake says, still surprised at the paycheck. "Usually we only got a hundred or less."

Some of that money went toward a good meal, as you might expect. But most of it was put aside for a move. Jake thought about how much Birmingham loved gospel singing. He had spent a lot of time there with John Daniel and he remembered how many other groups were making a living around that area.

Birmingham had been a hot town. There were the Radioaires, the Deep South Quartet and there was J. Daniel Williams and the Yellow Label Happy Hitters, which took their name from the syrup company that put them on the air.

With that military money in their pockets, they left South Carolina behind and got themselves a room for five at the Hillman Hotel in Birmingham.

*When they weren't selling their music, The
Melody Masters were selling pancake mix or
anything else that would pay the bills. With their
KFAB badges on their jackets are Lane Shaw,
Jake, Alvin Tootle and Wally Varner.*

It was almost like Jake remembered it. Birmingham did
love their music and other people in the business were also
beginning to notice them.

Half a century later, their nemesis from Florida—J.D.
Sumner offers a belated compliment. When others talk start
listing the most outstanding groups in history, Sumner mentions
Jake, Freeman, Tootle, Wetherington and Varner—his old ad-
versaries, the Melody Masters.

Once they were in Birmingham, they got a job singing on
WVOK radio. And yes, there were several groups working the
area, just like Jake had said. That was the problem. There were
too many groups and not enough places to sing. It wasn't long

before the money in their pockets when they came to town was gone.

And there were no peaches, either.

"We were just a bunch of kids. We thought we knew everything, but we didn't. We could sing, all right. But we didn't have one bit of business sense," Jake admits.

What the group needed—or so they decided—was a manager. They would select one in a democratic manner, by a vote.

"It would be a secret ballot," Jake says.

Cat Freeman, as talented as he was, was also a class clown. He had few serious thoughts in his head, on stage or off. When the other fellows thought about who should be their manager, they began to feel sorry for Freeman. Out of sympathy, they voted for him, figuring none of the other fellows would.

Freeman was elected—4 to 1.

Having a manager was not the solution though. Once again, they were about to become gospel gypsies. Pooling what money they could get together, they went into the radio station and recorded a number of transcriptions, which in the era before tapes were perfected was a radio station's best way of having a program. For a quartet, it was like their resume. They would have laughed if anyone had ever told them that nearly half a century later someone would come out with a forgotten copy of one of those transcriptions and that computer science would put another man's face on one of the Melody Masters.

That studio time gave them hope. Wherever you were, the sun always looked brighter somewhere else. Once more, they heard stories about how much work groups were getting elsewhere. This time the Promised Land was in the mid-west. The Blackwood Brothers had left the South for Iowa and other

The Melody Masters sang all over Nebraska. They sang a variety of music—not just gospel.

groups had followed. Armed with that kind of hope, the Melody Masters flooded the mail with their transcriptions, zeroing in on states they had never even visited.

Three offers came by return mail.

The most promising one was from KFAB a 50,000-watt radio station in Lincoln, Nebraska whose signal covered the state like a broadcast blanket. They offered the group an opportunity to become one of the station's 32 staff musicians. The Melody Masters called and said they were on their way.

First, they had to borrow some money.

Then they somehow had to get out of their hotel.

A plan was concocted.

Jake would stroll into the lobby and engage the desk clerk in a lively conversation. Meanwhile, Wetherington would sneak upstairs and cram into suitcases everything the other four guys had in the world.

That morning, the talk in the lobby covered everything from how hot the weather had been to how the Birmingham Barons had been playing.

For the Melody Masters, this was hardly the kind of exit they planned when they arrived in Alabama. Hope had turned into shame.

So while their lead singer kept the clerk busy in the front of the building, their bass singer was sneaking the luggage down the back stairs. Their old Buick was parked in back. The rest of the guys were waiting. A group of guys who usually had a lot to say were quiet that morning.

Management at KFAB wanted a quartet sound every day. They insisted that the Melody Masters have someone in the bullpen, ready to sing. Their six-man roster included Wally Varner, seated, Lane Shaw, Vernon Bright, Jake, Alvin Tootle and James Wethington.

Even today, Jake Hess is fond of saddle oxfords. He also was wearing them in Lincoln, Nebraska, when he and some of the other Melody Masters went shopping. He was joined by Lane Shaw, Alvin Tootle and James Wetherington.

The Melody Masters were going to Nebraska.

Their unpaid hotel bill was staying behind in Alabama.

"I guess those people at the hotel thought they would never see or hear from us again. But in a few weeks, as we began to do well, we sent money back there to pay that bill," Jake says.

They never talked much about that escapade and the others never knew that their honesty had been noticed. But many years later, after James Wetherington had died, some of his old friends went through a box filled with his personal papers.

By then, the Melody Masters had long since disbanded and the guys had gone their separate ways. But in Birmingham, they had been remembered. For among the stack of papers was a thank-you letter from the owner of the Hillman Hotel.

Out in Nebraska, far from the roots of themselves or their music., the Melody Masters began to sparkle. The money they were making was good and the music they were making was well received. But their development went beyond those factors.

With growing confidence and enough money in the bank to pay their bills, they were coming together as a quartet. A bunch of guys who weren't old enough to vote were learning responsibility, what it truly meant to be a Quartet Man.

Since they had no backing from any of the songbook companies, they could sing anything anyone wanted to hear and they were willing to try songs the traditional gospel groups stayed away from. They were getting some experimental material from Mosie Lister, their old baritone from Florida. And though none of them knew it at the time, they were developing individual personalities that would follow them for the rest of their time on gospel stages.

Varner was showing off at the keyboard, filling in the holes between the voices and becoming the "One Man Band" he still is today.

Freeman was becoming the class clown, playing the mischievous role that would always overshadow his God-given abilities as a tenor.

Wetherington was an instant favorite of the Nebraska audiences, with a bouncing bass style and the ability to turn a recitation into fun and meaning. Sometimes the women in the audience would even swoon when he sang.

Tootle was a gifted songwriter and a baritone who could make the others sound good. He alone was to remember Nebraska as his peak time as a gospel performer.

Jake, up to the time they went to the Midwest, had been a utility man, singing whatever part a quartet needed. Now he was learning about style and finesse, remembering the excitement Ernest Braswell had shown him.

They were drawing a salary from KFAB, enough that they didn't have to do evening concerts. But they did, and they immediately excited the Nebraska crowds who had never see a group so versatile. One minute they were creating a spiritual moment with an old hymn, the next they had folks on their feet with a foot-stomping spiritual and the next minute Jake might be crooning about a buttermilk sky.

"I still remember the words to Sioux City Sue," he says.

People from Lincoln to Omaha must have thought the quartet never slept, and they didn't much. They were on the air at 6:30 in the morning. They were back for the "Hi, Neighbor Show" at 9 o'clock, a 45-minute variety show that featured most to the station's staff musicians and singers. There was hardly time for a snack before it was time for their noontime gospel show.

The other musicians were strictly employees but the Melody Masters had wisely asked that they be allowed to deliver their "Be-Ats," which had always been a big part of a gospel group's radio show.

"You know, 'Tonight, we're going to be at the First Baptist Church.' Or else, 'Saturday, the boys will be at the high school gym.' Announcing your 'Be-Ats' was real important to you," Jake says.

The guys were even learning to handle their money. Wetherington bought a car of his own, one he didn't have to share with the group. Not that there was time for leisurely drives. They were busy making personal appearances or singing for their radio sponsors or they were doing a show at a county fair.

Keeping busy meant they were experimenting and expanding. The closest gospel quartet to them was the Blackwoods down the road in Iowa and they saw very little of them so they weren't playing off of others. They were becoming individuals. They weren't copying material or gimmicks because there was no one else to emulate. What they were doing was new and it was original.

"It was a good time for the group and it was good for me. All any of us ever wanted was a chance to sing gospel music and out in Nebraska that was what we were finally able to do. And we were making a living besides, something I had never really thought about. In my mind, I thought I would never leave Nebraska," Jake says.

It was 1948. He wouldn't be 21 years old until later that year, but Jake Hess was already a road warrior. He had covered a lot of miles and sung a lot of songs since he had left his tattered overalls behind in Haleyville. Out there in Nebraska, he thought his rainbow ended.

But across the country, down in Atlanta, Georgia, something was happening that would change those plans. Hovie Lister, one of gospel music's whiz kids, was putting together a group of his own. He had played piano with groups such as the LeFevre Trio, the Homeland Harmony Quartet and the Rangers.

For some time, he had been talking to his mentor, legendary bass singer, Big Jim Waits, about what he would do if he had his own quartet.

He wanted it to have style, to ooze class, to explode on a stage with more energy than a stick of dynamite and he wanted it to sound original, like no one else. He had a list of quartet people he would choose when the time was right to bring them together.

Hovie Lister even had a name.

The Statesmen Quartet.

Jake Hess knew nothing about these plans. But in Atlanta, Lister was putting them together. He got a job as a disc jockey on WCON, a radio station owned by The Atlanta Constitution, the city's morning newspaper and they wanted him to have a show featuring his new quartet.

Bobby Strickland, a gregarious tenor from Alabama would be a key member. He recommended his friend, Bervin Kendrick, for baritone. Mosie Lister, related to Hovie only by music, was the lead singer in those opening days. Gordon Hill was the bass singer, even though Hovie Lister wanted Waits or A.D. Soward, neither of whom were available.

They worked together in Atlanta, singing on the radio and getting to know one another by singing small jobs around town. Something was still missing.

Then, in the fall of 1948, Hovie Lister put in a call to Nebraska. He hardly knew the lead singer of the Melody Masters, but he knew about him. He offered him a job.

"It was a cut in pay," Jake says, "about $50 a week."

Something still intrigued him, however. He had heard about Hovie Lister. Everybody in the business had. He was probably the hottest item on anybody's list, on the stage and in the audience.

Jake called Herman Lister, his friend from Greenville. He definitely knew Hovie. He was his father. Jake had learned to trust this Christian gentleman and he listened to him more than he did his son.

"Go on down there, boy. Big things are coming. Big things are coming." And Herman Lister could not have imagined how right he would be.

Annual

ALL NIGHT
SING *and* CONCERT
December 4, 1948
CITY AUDITORIUM
MONTGOMERY, ALABAMA
8:00 P.M. Until 4 A.M.

Featuring the Nation's Finest Quartets, such as:

HOMELAND HARMONY, with "Big Jim Waits," of WAGA, Atlanta, Ga.

HAPPY HITTERS of WBRC, Birmingham, Ala.

THE STATESMEN QUARTET, with "Little Hovie Lister," of WCON, Atlanta, Ga.

HARMONY BOYS of WJJJ, Montgomery, Ala.

DIXIE RHYTHM QUARTET of WOOF, Dothan, Ala.

SUNSHINE BOYS, of WMAK, Nashville, Tenn.

THE SPEER FAMILY of WSIX, Nashville, Tenn., and Others.

ONE PRICE TO ALL. ADMISSION $1.00 PLUS 20c FED. TAX TOTAL $1.20

Tickets are on sale at GEO. JOHNSON SERVICE, Corner BIBB and MOULTON, MONTGOMERY, ALA. All Mail Orders to G. T. SPEER, 920 Sutton Hill Road, Nashville, Tenn.

Come, stay as long as you want to, leave when you get ready

——————DON'T MISS IT——————

4

Singing Like a Girl

Hovie Lister wondered what his father had gotten him into and so did Jake Hess. Nothing was said between them, not that words were needed. It was in the air the first time the Statesmen Quartet gathered in the studio at WCON. The piano player knew it and so did his new lead singer, but it was left to the tenor singer to deliver the message.

Bobby Strickland was already established in the quartet business, partly because of his emotional singing and partly because of his warm spirit. Like Jake, he came out of North Alabama. The two of them already felt comfortable with one another and the rotund tenor thought Jake needed to know that his job was on the line.

"Hovie doesn't like your singing. He thinks your voice is too thin," Strickland said. "He wants a big sound and he doesn't think you'll ever be able to do that. You have to do something or he's going to get rid of you."

What Strickland said confirmed what Jake already sensed. It wasn't something Lister had said. He had made no threats. On stage he was bragging about him. Yet, Jake could feel it, particularly during their rehearsals. Privately, he was saying that Jake sang like a girl.

Lister had wanted someone like Harley Lester of the Stamps Quartet whose voice seemed larger than life, along the lines of Strickland and Kendrick. That was also why he had wanted A.D. "Aycel" Soward, who posed for the group's original publicity photograph, even though Hill would be the bass singer when the group broke in.

"We felt we were at the beginning of something," Jake says. "I had given up what I came to know was the best job in gospel music to come there and I was determined to make it."

There may have been potential, but even that was hidden at first. The first booked job the group sang was in Monroe, Georgia, not far from the University of Georgia.

Their pay?

Each man received $11.53.

The group had gone on the radio October 18, 1948. Lister already had a 15-minute show on the station and on Sundays appeared with the LeFevre Trio, WCON's featured gospel group, on twice daily. All of the city's major outlets had a group—WAGA had the Homeland Harmony Quartet, WSB had the Sunshine Boys and the LeFevres were so popular that they also had a show on WGST, where the Harmoneers were featured.

With the support of the newspaper publisher's son, Lister had put together his group for WCON, owned by the Atlanta

When Jake Hess left his old friends behind in Nebraska, these fellows became his new friends. Hovie Lister, seated, had named the quartet even before they arrived. They were the Statesmen. Leaning over their piano player were Bobby Strickland, Jake, Gordon Hill and Bervin Kendrick. The group's first job out of Atlanta was in Monroe, Georgia, and Jake's share of their pay was broken down below.

Jake Hess		Gross Take	$78.30
		U.S. TAX	$13.05
	$11.53	Sponsor	$14.31
		Car	$6.30

Constitution. In the coming months, the paper helped promote this new singing group Lister organized and they had give them a send-off the Sunday before their program made its debut with an ad in which WCON celebrated "Our new Statesmen."

The quartet was on the air at 6:45 a.m. and 1:15 p.m. with a Sunday morning show at 8 a.m. Lister continued to spin records at 1:30 every afternoon. Their arrival inspired WGST to entice the LeFevres to join that station exclusively and they bought an ad that announced "the gospel darling," Eva Mae LeFevre, would have a daily shift as a disc jockey there.

Not even that $11.53 paycheck dampened Jake's optimism. In late November, when the group went into the studio to record for the Spivey Transcription series, his hopes were confirmed.

"I left there with a pocket full of money, more than I had ever had at one time. They paid us $500 each in cash, and those shows would be used on radio stations all over the country." he says.

Before 1948 ended, there was a December 4th All-Night Singing in Montgomery. The Speers lived there at that time and Pop Speer was putting together a big lineup. It would be the Statesmen's first major date and the billing was for "Little Hovie Lister and the Statesmen from WCON Radio in Atlanta, Georgia."

All the major groups were on hand, including the Home-land Harmony Quartet with Big Jim Waits, the Sunshine Boys and the Speers.

The other groups were intrigued by this new group that few of them had seen before. It was dominated by its tenor and its baritone. The lead singer was just another man on the stage. The bass singer was equally unknown. People responded though, which Jake credits to the reputation of their charismatic piano player.

"Hovie could have had four fence posts out there with him. He was that big. People just loved Hovie. From the time he

was 17 years old, he had been that big. Hovie sold himself by selling others. He couldn't get up in front of an audience and say how great he was, so he sold us. By saying how good I was, he made me better. I just didn't know how I could live up to what he said. I was insecure," Jake says.

One of the things Lister had wanted was a quartet that looked like it could sing, one with class. That meant dressing with style so they went to Bremen, Georgia, and bought matching suits, direct from a manufacturer. They still weren't happy with the way they looked, however.

"A.D. Soward was with us by then and he went and borrowed the money himself so we could have some suits made. We got them from Glenn McNair, down near the radio station on Forsyth Street. He made suits for the Statesmen from then on," Jake says.

Lister had noticed that quartet members had a tendency to show up with a mismatched tie or shirt or a scuffed pair of shoes. As they built up their wardrobe, he would make sure every man knew what to wear. To be in that group, you had to live up to an image. Even today, those who know him will say you never see Hovie Lister without a suit and tie.

"We were Statesmen—which I still think is the greatest name for a quartet anybody ever came up with. That was Hovie.

A.D. "Aycel" Soward, left, soon joined the group on bass. It was Soward who floated a loan and bought the Statesmen their first tailored suits. He was part of a group that included Jake, Bobby Strickland, Bervin Kendrick and Hovie Lister.

James Wetherington, right, was rescued from Nebraska to sing bass. Not long after he joined the group, Lee Roy Abernathy helped christen him "The Big Chief." One by one, the quartet that was to become a legend was coming together.

He had everything in mind before he talked to anybody. He had a natural ability to put a group together. He wasn't just another motivator, another funny guy at the piano or a preacher. He was all things and more. He was a master," Jake says.

As a group, they were beginning to jell. Within four months, Hill had moved on and Soward, who had worked with both Lister and Strickland in the past, joined the group. He didn't stay long, however, only a few months after he put up the money for those suits. And in the spring of 1949, when the

When Hovie Lister went into the Army, the Statesmen took on a new look. Doy Ott, second from the right, played piano. The rest of the group were Jake, baritone Troy Posey, James Wetherington and tenor Earl Terry. Once Lister was back, Ott moved over to baritone and became valuable as a singer and an arranger.

*If you were going to be a Statesman, you had to dress
like a Statesman. Cat Freeman discovered that when
he replaced Bobby Strickland. With his arrival, three
of the Melody Masters from Nebraska were together
again and this time they would not have to steal
peaches in order to have something to eat.*

group again needed a bass singer, Jake insisted they hire his
close friend Wetherington, who was still in Nebraska.

Lister gave in this time. He had always respected the
Melody Masters and today says they were a group that was
ahead of its time. But in 1949, he wasn't sure he wanted so

much stage movement and nobody had as much as the suave but flamboyant Wetherington, a man who could dominate a stage.

Not long after Wetherington arrived, the group was singing in Donaldsonville, Georgia. Lee Roy Abernathy heard Lister introduce his bass singer as James Wetherington.

"He's part Indian, isn't he? Make him your Big Chief." Abernathy suggested.

The next night, when Lister introduced the group, when he got to his bass singer, he was the Big Chief.

And from that night on, he was.

The Statesmen were taking shape, but Jake knew Lister still wasn't sure about the lead singer. He had tried a couple of voice coaches in Atlanta but both of them wanted to turn him into a Nelson Eddy, or into a singer who might be a candidate for The Metropolitan Opera. Finally, someone recommended John Hoffman, director of the Atlanta Civic Opera and the head of the Baptist Radio Hour. After several months on a waiting list, Jake finally went in for an appointment with Hoffman.

"I want to sing like me," Jake told him from the outset. "So if you can teach me to sing the way I'm trying to sing, I can pay you. But I can't pay you if you are going to break me down and make me sound like some opera singer."

"If you want to throw your money away, then I will take it," Hoffman said, promising to listen to the Statesmen on radio the very next morning.

At 2 o'clock the next afternoon, Jake hurried from the radio show and arrived at Hoffman's studio for their first session. He was anxious to hear what the teacher said since he had never heard either the quartet or his newest pupil.

"I must say, you sound just like a little girl," Hoffman said.

Hoffman was laughing at him. Jake had been trying to make a living as a singer for nearly five years by then and he

Guitars were almost a novelty on Southern gospel stages. Only a few groups used them in the early 1950s. Sometimes Jake would get out the guitar and play along with Hovie. Here they were rehearsing a song for their daily radio program.

had been going to singing conventions all of his life. Now this man was telling him that he needed to broaden his tone and quit singing like a little girl.

Hoffman laughed at him that first afternoon and left the surprised student more than little embarrassed, but he would be Jake Hess' teacher for the next eight years.

"Dr. Hoffman was right. I didn't know anything," Jake says, remembering how he felt when this stranger criticized him for something others had always praised. "I had gone to other teachers and most of them would start me as an advanced student and I knew nothing. Singing was just something I did. He didn't want me to be so precise in my pronunciation, which I had gotten from Pop who told me to say every word. Dr. Hoffman gave me a bad time about words but I would remind him that I only wanted to perfect what I was doing. I wanted to sing like me."

Lister must have noticed the results of these sessions, but nothing was said. "Hovie knew about my lessons, but I don't know if he ever knew that Bobby had told me that he was displeased with me," Jake says.

As a singer and as a person, he was developing.

Jake credits Hovie Lister.

"He was the main reason I started taking my singing seriously. When I found out he was going to get rid of me, I started working harder. I didn't realize I was coming up with any particular style. I wasn't copying. I wasn't trying to sing any particular way. I was just evolving," he says.

He was defining the style that became his trademark and so was the Statesmen Quartet. In reality, so was all of Southern gospel music.

From the beginning, it had been a genre of music that defied definition. You just knew it when you heard it. The four-part harmony. The rolling piano. The feeling. The message that spread the Word in an evangelical style. It had come out of churches and out of those dinner-on-the-grounds singing conventions. But as the Statesmen came together in 1948, the music was coming to town.

Gospel music's beginnings could be traced back to Dwight Moody, a powerful evangelist of the late 1800s. He introduced the music and a series of Sunday School songbooks followed, using songs that were more youthful than the staid hymnals of that time.

Before he was old enough to vote, Hovie Lister was a dominant figure in gospel music. When he went to a microphone, he owned that audience. He could have been a greater piano player, but sometimes he enjoyed messing up so he could laugh at himself.

The Jake Hess "Style."

As the shaped note schools grew in the early 1900s and James D. Vaughan moved to Tennessee, the business of music grew. Putting out two songbooks a year, Vaughan was selling 85,000 copies a year as early as 1912. In the 1930s, joined in the publishing field by his alumni, V.O. Stamps and J.R. Baxter, they sold 5 million song books.

Vaughan had quartets scattered all over the country, some working directly for him and scores of groups singing his music and pushing his books.

Then, when the Depression generation came home from the war, the balance of influence changed. Instead of the publishing companies being seen as the gospel messengers, it was the quartets that sang the music that began to dominate. The quartets began singing the songs the way they wanted to sing them, not note-by-note the way the song writers and publishers wanted them sung.

To some, it was country music gone to church, but it was really an amalgamation of many kinds of music, from the spirituals of the black churches to the close harmonies of a very white singing group like the Four Aces.

Definitions vary.

"Quartets put their own stamp on things. Trace a Southerner's musical roots and it always goes back to gospel. It

Bervin Kendrick, above with glasses, left to join Bobby Strickland and the Crusaders. Doy Ott, rubbing his head below, took over as the baritone and soon became a Statesmen mainstay.

What a flamboyant lineup this edition of the Statesmen was. With Hovie Lister banging the keys and jumping up on the piano, Big Chief showing off on bass, Sister Cat Freeman on tenor and Jake rolling his eyes, only Doy Ott stood still, hardly disturbing the crease in his pants.

was our grounding, and this music comes closer to being the most complete merger of music that I can imagine," says Dr. Wayne Flynt, a historian at Auburn University.

"It has aspects of culture, music and religion. Our beliefs are so public. We're oral, whether it is a preacher in the pulpit, a politician on the stump or a singer. Our religious culture is to share the word, and singing is such an effective way to do this," says Dr. Charles Reagan Wilson, of the University of

Mississippi's Center for the Study of Southern Culture and co-editor of The Encyclopedia of Southern Culture.

"It was a reflection of the working class ethos," says Dr. Charles Wolfe, a professor of English at Middle Tennessee State University.

"It was an outpost of American society and after World War II, it gave the people who had moved to town a chance to touch base with their rural roots," says Don Cussed, a music professor at Belmont University.

The Statesmen were beginning just as those people who had come home from the war were getting settled. Many of them had flocked to cities like Atlanta, Birmingham, Nashville and Memphis, leaving behind the farms on which they had grown up. Quartets were moving with them, to take advantage of the population, the radio audiences and, increasingly, the record industry.

From singing conventions at small country churches, gospel music was spreading its wings and becoming a major part of life all over the South, in the small towns and in the big cities. The people who sang the songs were becoming stars as well as people who sang about the Lord. Their influence would spread—even to Tupelo, Mississippi, where a teenaged Elvis Presley was begging his folks to take him to gospel singings.

All of that was still in the future when Jake Hess arrived from Nebraska. Atlanta was a town trying to see if it was big enough to wear long pants. In many ways, it was still an over-grown country town.

Phones could still be dialed with six numbers and the local exchanges still answered to names like Fairfax and Calhoun. Politicians were raising money for a multi-lane high-way through town. You could catch a three-hour flight for New York but most people preferred to go to Union Station and get a seat on the Silver Comet. The newspaper advertised the radio listings but in a few months would begin publishing the city's limited television listings, an event that would be very important in the future of the Statesmen.

It was an exciting time to be in that city and an exciting time to be in gospel music. For the Statesmen Quartet, it was also exciting. Hovie Lister was booking them in places you would need a magnifying glass to locate on a Georgia map.

Jake was finding his dream and he was finding success. As he did, he wanted to share it with his parents. Knowing that his parents had never owned a home, he bought them one in Haleyville, Alabama. This particular night, William Stovall and Lydia Hess were his guests at a Christmas party given for the Statesmen by RCA Victor.

Their ritual was back-breaking. They would do their morning show on WCON, walk to breakfast together, come back for their midday show, then go into lengthy rehearsals.

In the evenings, they usually were on the road for a date somewhere in the state, packing into a Plymouth coupe, with their 265-pound tenor singer taking up more than his share of room.

Lister was always telling them he knew so many people and he could talk anyone into spreading the word about the group. That evolved into a favorite game they used to pass the time. It also made radio listeners think this quartet must have had a show on every station in the state.

"Bet you can't get us on a radio station in this town?" they would taunt Lister as they neared a town. He was as competitive as they were so following the tower, he would pull up in front of the local station.

Lister was fearless and he was a salesman. It wouldn't be long before he would motion the guys inside for an impromptu 15-minute broadcast. He enjoyed living up to their dares.

"I hate to tell him, but in the backseat we were making wagers," Jake laughs.

But while groups such as the Statesmen were wearing out tires traveling to any town that had a church or an auditorium, Wally Fowler was concocting an idea that was going to make even more changes in 1948.

Fowler was also a graduate of the John Daniel Quartet and he said the idea for his All-Night Singings came from V.O. Stamps, who was the backer for that group when Fowler sang with them.

By 1948, he was a member of the Oak Ridge Quartet, the gospel forerunner of today's country-pop group. He decided to put together a package of the more popular groups and advertise they would be singing until the sun came up.

His first one was in November of that year at the Ryman Auditorium in Nashville. It was successful and soon he was booking them all over the Southeast.

"I've seen groups show up that Wally hadn't even thought of," Jake says. "I heard Wally ask one group what they were doing there and the guy said 'Look at our book. You asked us to be here.' Wally put them on the show and paid them."

The Statesmen became one of Wally Fowler's major attractions. they became regulars and as the popular groups joined him, WSM Radio in Nashville agreed to put an hour of the show from the Ryman on the air. This was a big step for Fowler since their signal extended all over the country.

Gospel music would never again be the same. There was still a place for the traditional shows in the small halls. But quartets were now making regular stops at all of the major auditoriums.

As the music grew, so did the Statesmen. But they were also undergoing changes. Hovie Lister went into the Army and Doy Ott sat in on piano, later to replace Bervin Kendrick as the baritone. Bobby Strickland left to start the Crusaders Quartet and three years after organizing his own group he was killed in a tragic auto accident, just days after agreeing to become the spokesman for the Florida Citrus Commission. Cat Freeman by then a member of the Blackwood Brothers, stepped in as the tenor in 1950, bringing with him the foolishness he had begun to show on stage with the Melody Masters.

In two years, they had become important members of the gospel music family. Herman Lister had promised big things were coming. Quickly they had come. Only for Jake Hess and the other members of The Statesmen, the biggest things were yet to happen.

Jake Hess and the former Joyce McWaters cut the cake on their wedding day—October 5, 1952.

Joyce and Jake were married in her family's living room. Mosie Lister was best man for the ceremony and his wife, Wylene, was the only person from Atlanta who came to Alabama. Even now, he says she is his "only friend."

When Jake was away, Joyce had to be both mother and father. But when he came home, they turned everything into a family activity—even the time they spent in the kitchen.

week, he would send money to Pop. The more he made, the more he sent. Finally, he was able to buy the first house they ever owned. He even bought a refrigerator that plugged into the wall instead of one you had to load with blocks of ice.

For years, he had been wandering all over the country, spending more time hearing the buzz of a car engine than anything else. Atlanta had been the first place he had reached out to folks.

Mosie and Wylene Lister had become a family for him. He had known Mosie in Florida. They were both former Melody Masters. They had renewed their friendship since the creation of the Statesmen.

On a Sunday, after the guys got in late the night before, Jake would get up and go to their house. The Listers had twin daughters that he adored. For Brenda and Barbara, he was a Santa Claus and an Easter Bunny. When he got married, they were jealous. They wanted Jake all for themselves.

Jake's plans never really included getting married. He was obsessed with his dream of singing gospel music. He knew what it took to do that. This was an era when it meant three radio shows a day and an appearance somewhere just about every night. And if you were a Statesmen, there were also re-hearsals. All of this, he shared with Joyce.

"I knew exactly what I was getting into. He told me all of that, and I had seen the quartets come through. I knew what kind of life it was. But I knew he had to sing," she says.

They were married in her parents' living room. Mosie Lister was best man so he had to be there. Wylene did not, but she was the only guest who came over from Atlanta.

"I tell her she is my only friend," Jake says.

"He still calls her 'Friend,' even now," Mosie laughs.

They were married October 5, 1952. And somewhere around this time, Jake told Joyce about Becky Phillips.

She was a woman in his past, one he has never forgotten. It has been more than 50 years since they met and he hasn't seen her since 1946 but she's still a special person to him.

The Daniel Quartet, Troy Daniel's group, had gone to Florence, Alabama, to rehearse. Through the connections of their manager Jud Phillips and his brother Sam, the group got a show on WREC in Memphis. Sam Phillips would later found Sun Records in Memphis but back then he was just a shy, awkward radio DJ.

In Florence, Jake again saw Sam's wife, Becky. They had met when he was known as "Curly," when his hair came from God and not the store. He had been singing with the Rhythm Rascals and they did a show on WLAY in Sheffield. This both scared and excited the sharecropper's kid from Haleyville.

"She would tell me how to get better sound. There was one microphone and I didn't know a thing about mikes. She could tell I was scared to death. She showed me how to stand, what to do. She was real sweet to me," he says.

He was 14 years old when he met her. She gave him a tour of the station, even taking him into the inner sanctum, the announcer's booth. Intuitively sensing he needed a boost in confidence, she bragged on his singing.

Even then, she was important to him.

"She took up time with me, and time is precious," he says. "All of that is no big deal to most people, but it sure was with me."

And still is.

"I guess she made more of an impression on me than anyone in my life. She was so sweet and perfect. I swore all of those years ago that if I got married, I was going to have a little girl and name her Becky."

Jake and Joyce had that little girl on September 11, 1953.

Her name is Becky.

Joyce Hess remembers the day Jake showed up at home wearing his toupee for the first time. Their children don't remember a time when their dad didn't have his head covered.

Chris, named for his dad's brother, was born December 27, 1955 and Jake Jr. came along on June 25, 1960.

Although their routine was different, Jake and Joyce tried to make it a normal life, even though the children were forever waving good-bye to a face behind the window of a bus.

"That was Joyce. She did all of that. I can take no credit for all our kids have become," he says.

"It was a balancing act. I had to be their mother and their father when he was gone. Then, when he was home, I had to let him be their daddy," she says.

When Becky was born, Jake was in Texas. He didn't see her until she was eight days old. By then, folks at the hospital thought Dick Ruiz, Hovie Lister's brother-in-law, was Becky's father.

After the kids were born, when he was home, every day was a picnic. If Jake went to the cleaners, they went to the cleaners. If Jake had to load the bus, they cleaned the bus. If Jake went to the post office, so did the kids.

Becky and a pooch got acquainted at the old Atlanta airport.

Before Becky was born, Jake told Joyce what he wanted to name their daughter. She was named for Becky Phillips, whose husband Sam discovered Elvis Presley. Mrs. Phillips helped make Jake comfortable on one of his first radio jobs.

*If Jake was home, the Hess Family was usually together. They
tried to make fun out of simple things.*

Jake Jr. forgot to close his eyes but he remembered to say his bedtime prayers along with Becky and Chris.

"We didn't plan things. Everybody would just hit the car and off we would go," Jake says.

"When Dad came home, we had so much fun. Mother and Daddy together were always fun and happy," Becky says, looking back at the days when her father was either coming back or about to leave.

"It was a trade-off," Chris says. "When he was home, he was home. He might not be home at 5 o'clock every day and we might not see him for several days. But when he came in we might see him every day, all day for three or four days."

Fridays and Saturdays were a special treat. They got to go to the auditorium where their daddy was singing. Becky says they grew so accustomed to this that they took it for granted. In many ways, they were going to the office with him but it was an office where they got to stay up until 3 in the morning.

"It was more fun than an office. An office didn't have popcorn and hot dogs and hallways going up and up, going this

*When Joyce and Jake went to the studio for a family portrait,
Jake Jr. showed he had one of his father's habits along with his
name as those fingers around his chin indicate.*

way and that way. You could go up there and hide and nobody
would know where you were," Jake Jr. says.

They were around the auditoriums, around the singers
and around the music. That also meant they were around the
fans. Many still remind them of that.

"I remember you. I remember you being brought up on
stage one time and you were wearing your pajamas. They had a
hole in them," Chris laughs, repeating a story he has been told
many times.

At home, there were games to play. Maybe it was simple
Christmas ornaments that needed making. Maybe it was a back-

yard basketball game that put their father on crutches for several weeks.

"You came down on his foot, didn't you, Jake."

"No, Chris, it was you."

His foot hurt but Jake kept on playing. After they quit, it still hurt but he figured he would walk away the soreness. Three days later, he went to the doctor. It was broken and he came home with a big cast and a pair of crutches.

"We had some steps leading up to the foyer and every day he would fall. He would laugh at himself and the next time he would fall again. It got to where we were standing there ready to catch him," Chris says.

Of course, there was music.

Even a dog that was a ham. They still laugh about a dachshund they had that would sing the National Anthem as a duet with Joyce.

If Joyce Hess sang the National Anthem, their dog, Snoopy, would join right in. However, Snoopy used neither his eyes nor his paws when he sang.

Jake's parents were always an important part of his life. Lydia Hess died in 1956 and William Stovall Hess passed away in 1963.

Their father was a star, but not to them. For his children, he was just Dad. But when your father makes records, has his picture in the newspaper and is on television, these are the things your friends at school can't help but notice. That was especially true in Nashville where in later years he had a daily television show.

Jake Jr. remembers a friend at the University of Tennessee who every time he saw him would hum the theme song to his father's TV show. He was given something his sister and brother were not. He was Jake Hess, Jr.

"There wasn't anything negative about it, really. Of course, when I cash a check sometimes people will say, 'Are you related to the famous Jake Hess?' But of course, his name is really W. Jake Hess," the younger version says.

After going through all of the shenanigans with his own name, his father stuck him with W. Jake Hess Jr.

"What does the 'W' stand for, people would ask. Nothing. Teachers would ask me, 'What does it stand for?' Nothing. Even graduating from high school, they wanted to know. Nothing. It is W. Jake," he says.

He realizes that if he had been a singer himself, the name would have carried another significance. "I would have had to change my name—to W maybe."

Becky remembers more of the Statesmen years than her brothers and she also remembers when she realized how much he was loved by gospel music fans. She had always been around concerts and singings and this particular night was in Memphis, at the National Quartet Convention. Her father had had his first heart attack and he was returning to the stage. The family was backstage watching.

"People were swarming around him. Lights were flashing. People were applauding. I thought, 'Gosh, they love him. They really love him.' You could see it and you could feel it," she says.

Most kids think their father is special. It's part of being a kid. And these children were no different. "Being a special dad is more important than people rushing a stage. We wouldn't care what he did—truck driver, milkman, whatever. He would still be special to us. He is Dad," Chris says.

There was also another side to their lives. Most children have sole possession of their parents. Becky, Chris and Jake Jr.

Mosie and Wylene Lister's twin daughters, Brenda and Barbara, were "Jake's kids" until his own children were born. Later he helped them try a musical career of their own. Even now, he can't tell them apart.

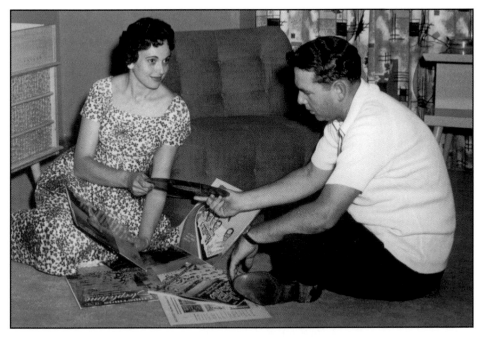

When Joyce and Jake got married, she was working in a record store in Gadsden, Alabama. In later years, she helped him with some of the Statesmen's musical ventures.

had to share their father with an audience that could at times be possessive itself.

Sandy Meador thought she was Jake's girl. She was growing up in New Albany, Mississippi, when the Statesmen started coming through there on their way to Memphis. When they came, her folks took her to every concert.

"When I heard that he had his own little girl, I was devastated. I thought he wouldn't love me anymore. I was jealous. A few years ago, when I kept pestering Becky to see how he was after heart surgery, I told her about this. She was real sweet about it," Meador says.

Sometimes, Becky, Chris and Jake Jr. were not just the singer's kid, they were also the singer's audience. When she

This scene was repeated too often for Jake and Joyce. For Quartet Men had to stay on the road in order to sing their music.

was young, Becky used to wonder when the quartet was going to sing "Get Away, Jordan." She liked it when they did silly things. Once they were older, they learned what he was singing about.

"I was in California with him, when he sang with the Imperials. It was in a school auditorium, during a rehearsal, when the reality of it struck me. I had flopped down on the back row when it dawned on me that this wasn't just music. For me, it moved from entertainment to ministry," Chris says.

Jake Hess Jr. isn't old enough to remember the Statesmen but as a grownup he has a collection of their records that he treasures.

Now the three of them are grown. Becky is the wife of Brent Buck, a businessman in Columbus, Georgia. They have four children—Emmy Shea, Brent, Lauren and Ansley.

Chris and Cindy Hess also live in Columbus. He is the minister of youth at Wynnbrook Baptist Church, which has become the home church of the entire family. He and Cindy have three children—Casey Jake, Natalie and Megan.

Jake Jr. has opened a landscaping business there and tends his garden in Juniper, Georgia, a short drive from Columbus.

Becky moved to Georgia when she and Brent were married in 1992. Jake and Joyce knew they would be burning up the highway between Nashville and Columbus since Emmy Shea and little Brent would be there. So when Jake decided to leave the road a final time, he and Joyce also moved. The others came one by one.

"We are a close family, a unique family. I see so many dysfunctional families and I see that Dad and Mom provided a stable family. In today's world, that is unique. They are Christian parents, not Christian superstars," Chris says.

At the same time, they recognize that their father is also a legend in the eyes of so many people. Jake Jr., who doesn't remember the Statesmen, has studied their work. He watched videos and has an extensive collection of 78 records.

"I like them and I don't like all of the gospel music I hear. I like their movement, their rhythm. America was just coming out of the Big Bank era and it was before rock 'n' roll. There was Hovie with long greasy hair and Dad jumping up on a piano. They were doing this innovative stuff that was before its time. The influence Dad has had on music—directly and indirectly—you can't measure. People who watched and listened to them may not realize how much of an influence they were," Jake Jr. says.

But don't ask Chris what it is like to be the son of a superstar. "I know he's had an effect on the world. But to me he is real, not someone on a stage. He's just plain Dad."

*"Get Away, Jordan," people want to cross over and see
Jake and Hovie go from sweet harmony to a frantic stage.*

6

Even Perfection Must End

People who saw the Statesmen Quartet have a tape player in their mind. They push a button and replay the images. Some were in Atlanta, in an auditorium where Caruso sang and wrestlers groaned. Some sat in rickety old pews at the Ryman in Nashville. Some were at the Ellis Auditorium in Memphis. Some were in a high school gymnasium, with a basketball goal cranked high above the stage.

But the image was the same. Jake with his fat eyes. Hovie vaulting on first the bench, then the piano. Chief, his knees rocking and his rhythm like a metronome. Doy just blending, never moving enough to disturb the crease in his trousers. Denver with his classy sound. Rosie adding a pinch of soul to the recipe.

*When the spirit moved him, Hovie Lister would
leave a piano playing to Doy Ott and join Denver
Crumpler, Jake and James Wetherington on
songs like "The Old Landmark."*

Turn up the sound. It might be a Mosie Lister song,
something with happy rhythm or maybe the memory of meeting
the master. Whatever the song, it echoes even now, every
change of chord, every phrase so precise that the voices sound
like one.

"The Statesmen had it all. We had a quartet for radio, for
television, for records, for publishing, for special events. We
enjoyed singing and we enjoyed rehearsing. We worked at what

we did. One time in Chicago, a magazine had called us a side show. Hovie said we were not a side show. We were the main attraction," Jake Hess says.

He's proud and he admits he is partial. Given that, he doesn't have to ponder a question about the personnel he would recruit if he could put a gospel quartet together of singers past and present—assuming that he would sing lead.

"If we're talking about singing, I don't know if I would change the personnel of the Statesmen ... Hovie, Chief, Doy and Denver. And if Denver wasn't available, then Rosie, for he added, he didn't take away."

Others in gospel music agree.

George Younce is one. In many ways, the organizational makeup of the Cathedrals is patterned after the Statesmen. His hero, naturally was James Wetherington, the Chief. When he talks about him, he goes in and out of an impersonation of the late bass singer that is right on target. Younce sounds like a fan as he remembers that group.

"The Statesmen were better than we remember them. I've never seen five men walk out on stage and create such an aura. There was a charisma about each one of them. Their personalities just flashed! The Big Chief, gosh, I'd be singing with someone like the Blue Ridge Quartet and I'd run get a front row seat. Man, he tore me up. My eyes were absolutely glued on him. I knew what everybody else was doing, but my eyes couldn't get off of him. I can hear him now, 'Jubilee's a comin, it's a comin' in the mornin ...' Doy Ott. I don't guess I ever came up to him without hugging. There weren't any words said, we just hugged each other's neck. It wasn't 'I love you, Doy' or 'I love you, George,' we could just feel our hearts say that. And Hovie, when he would sit at the piano and rear back and holler, I wanted to jump up out of my seat and run. Denver Crumpler,

When Denver Crumpler came over from the Rangers in 1953, he joined a group that gospel historians say was "the perfect quartet."

man alive, I'd say how you feeling? He'd say I'm hoarse as a jaybird. Then he would walk out and sound like a mockingbird. He was incredible. Rosie Rozell came along and he just blew the roof off of gospel music. So different. Jake, all of the other lead singers wanted to sing like him and the truth of the matter was, everybody did, for a number of years. It got boring to hear fellows trying to sing like Jake Hess. Get your own style, I thought, give me a break. It used to make me mad because Jake is Jake, there hasn't been another one and there never will be."

Only Jake and Hovie Lister survive. The group is part of history. Yet, to Younce, they should be a textbook for people today who want to sing.

"Guys who walk out on the stage and think they're doing something new or original ... now or in the future ... pardon me, it's been done. Whatever you think you do that is original, let me tell you, The Statesmen have done it and done it better than anybody else will ever do it," Younce says.

He was remembering the energy created on a stage, but there was more to the Statesmen than the music or the gospel message they delivered. They were also an industry unto themselves.

Their syndicated television show for Nabisco showed others how television could be used. They created a record company and a publishing company so they could control their own destiny. They forged a relationship with the Blackwoods, developing a rivalry that became a marriage. They helped bring gospel concerts from the courthouse into the arenas with what someone said was "Broadway Gospel," referring to the classy image that Lister demanded, down to the idea that even loading the bus, they should look like Statesmen.

"God just blessed us—in so many ways," Jake says.

So much of it began with the arrival in 1953 of Denver Crumpler. No one thought he would ever leave the Rangers. He

Sometimes they were hobos riding the rails. Sometimes they were cowboys riding the range. Sometimes they were riding in old cars or on the golf course. The Statesmen never knew what the set or the costumes would be for the Nabisco Show.

was a fixture. Lister and Ott knew him from their stints with the quartet so Lister made the call.

The free-spirited Cat Freeman, remembered more for his comedy than his under-rated tenor voice, was leaving and to the surprise of everyone in the quartet world, Denver Crumpler joined Jake, Hovie, Chief and Doy.

Mosie Lister was a member of this team who seldom was introduced as a member of the starting lineup. First, he was valuable as a creative arranger. Then came a string of songs that established him as one of gospel music's premiere songwriters.

Theirs was a unique relationship. He sat in on the rehearsals. He was their friend. They were together when songs were written, arranged and performed. Mosie would be around the piano, throw out an idea, and soon the idea would be a song. Many were written with specific voices in mind.

Most of the time, it was Jake.

"I put down the words and Jake provided the expression and the feelings. Vocally, he supplied the emotion I was feeling. I put down the words and the music and his voice and personality took over. When I would hear him I would think 'That was what I was thinking,' even though I couldn't do it with my voice. Jake would do it instinctively. Those things could not have happened if we hadn't been close friends and maybe if we hadn't lived in the same town. It's important for a writer to know a singer's personality. I learned what he enjoyed singing and I tried to write those kinds of songs. Even words he would enjoy. I knew how he would color it, roll it, twist it," Mosie Lister says.

His relationship with Jake and with the quartet turned out songs that became gospel classics. Not that they always agreed on what was good.

"I was wrong at times. When Mosie wrote 'How Long Has It Been?' I said it was good, but not for the Statesmen. We were into 'Happy Rhythm,' 'Jubilee's a Comin' and 'Oh, My Lord, What a Time.' Then he brings us that and it had no enthusiasm. But you can see that he was right and I was wrong. That's why he's the songwriter and I'm the singer," Jake says.

This was the team that ventured into syndicated television network. The group had a local show on WSB-TV in Atlanta and Lister sold the National Biscuit Company on not only gospel music but his group's ability to sell crackers.

Nabisco created record boxes that looked like saltine cracker boxes. When the group would go into a town, the local salesman would have product to display on stage.

"They're my kind of eating," Hovie Lister would tell folks, and they would listen.

Instead of putting four men and a piano in front of the camera, their show was a production. There were sets, props and costumes. Sound tracks for the show were pre-recorded, which meant the group had to lip-sync the lyrics. The vocals were recorded at the Biltmore Hotel ballroom. The quartet would go in there about midnight and as the customers said good night, they began setting up.

Music was provided by Wade Creger and his orchestra. On stage, Hovie Lister was their orchestra. On television, there was even a horn section.

The wailing horns helped get them into a controversy that ended up with several DJs—including Warren Roberts in Atlanta—breaking their record on the air. The song was "Headin' Home." The fellows were dressed like hobos and as Jake's solo ended, a mournful horn could be heard.

"A sinful horn," Jake laughs.

Did they ever confront the DJs?

"No, we couldn't have paid for better publicity," Jake says. The controversy meant more people would be tuning in which delighted the Nabisco people.

Through the years with Jake Hess: The hair, the hands and the smile.

They had been concerned with Jake before, not about horns but about his style. An early letter writer talked about his "fat eyes," and the producer was always cautioning him about raising his hands in the air. They feared his hands would block someone's face. Finally a representative of Nabisco's advertising agency, McCann-Erickson, took him aside during a rehearsal, with a new suggestion.

Bill Harrison had drawn the short straw and he was elected to talk to Jake about his hair, or rather his increasing lack of hair. Harrison was stumbling and bumbling but Jake could see where the conversation was going.

"Bill, you buy it and I'll wear it," Jake said, and walked away. Nabisco could make Vanilla Wafers and this time they made a head of hair. The first time he wore it on stage was in Macon, Georgia—a town that knew little about store-bought hair.

"Jake thought it was going to fall off in the lap of somebody on the front row," Lister says. "He was nervous."

Making their entrance as usual, the Statesmen quickly did a couple of their signature tunes. Denver had taken a lead and Chief took the mike for a solo. So far, nothing from Jake. A man in the balcony noticed this and decided to let the leader of the group know.

"Brother Hobie, let the kid with the wig sing," the man screamed.

His hairpiece has become as much a trademark as the gestures he makes with his hands or the way his active eyes seem to harmonize with his voice. He has grown older but his hair has grown younger.

Sandy Meador was a child in New Albany, Mississippi, when Jake's new hair made its debut. Her mother would take her to the record counter to visit her favorite singer and he would always set her up on the table.

When Jake was relaxing on the cattle farm he bought in Alabama, no one cared about his hair. On television, they did.

"He picked me up and I thought, 'What is this?' In a little town like New Albany you didn't know about toupees. I can still feel the expression that came on my face. It was in a knot. I remember how that one kind of curled up into a knot in the front," says Meador, who now lives near Atlanta.

Mickey Vaughn is another long-time fan. She has a hat he wore when the group went cowboy on TV. She also has a hair-piece that reached retirement age.

"I just asked for it," says Vaughn a real estate agent in Dallas, Texas. Once a year, she carefully packs up Jake's old hair and carries it to Greenville, South Carolina, for promoter Charlie Waller's Grand Old Gospel Reunion show. It is worn in a skit where someone portrays a singer who resembles Jake Hess. The identity is unknown.

From their beginning in 1948, the Statesmen Quartet was a group that copied no one. They had their own brand of harmony and excitement. Above is a business card with the group pictured on the back. That's Jake Hess, Rosie Rozell, Doy Ott and The Big Chief, James Wetherington. Hovie Lister, the founder and piano player is seated. Below is a typical memory of the Statesmen captured on stage at the Quartet Convention in Memphis.

After leaving the Statesmen, Jake started the Imperials. They introduced a new sound and they also introduced a band with drums. This isn't the original lineup but it was a talented one that included Gary McSpadden, Armond Morales, Jim Murray, Joe Moscheo and Jake.

The Sound of Youth also was memorable for Jake since he sang with two of his children. Starting with Jake, his son Chris, Lee Petrucci, Mike Kinser, Doc Stone and his daughter Becky.

When the Hess family is together, there are always smiles. The smiles in this picture were inspired by Becky's wedding to Brent Buck in 1992. Helping give her away were Chris, Jake Jr., Joyce and her proud Dad. But when he isn't dressed up, Jake enjoys spoiling his grandchildren. That's Casey Jake checking to see if there's hair under his grandfather's cap and you know that Brent needs his help with that ear of corn.

There have been too many good-byes when Jake had to board a bus. There have been too many days spent in hospitals while Jake fought his "isms." But through it all, his family has survived. The smile on Jake's face shows the love he has for Casey Jake and "little" Brent. Pictured below is the entire family, Joyce, Daughter Becky, sons Chris and Jake Jr., son-in-law Brent Buck, daughter-in-law Cindy, grandchildren Emmy Shea, Brent, Casey Jake, Natalie, Megan, Lauren and Ansley.

"It's not me. It's my brother," says Lily Fern Weatherford of the Weatherfords, a long-time friend of Jake's.

His son, Chris Hess, often joins his father for duets and has to stress that Jake is his father, not his brother. It might have something to do with the fact that Chris, the minister of youth at Wynnbrook Baptist Church in Columbus, Georgia, has less hair than his father.

"What God has not wrought, Dad has bought," Chris says.

Others also have bought, which is noted by Mark Lowry, who sings and jokes with the Gaither Vocal Band.

"If the Rapture comes during the National Quartet Convention, nothing is going to be left behind but an arena full of hair," Lowry says.

Whether or not Jake Hess' new look had anything to do with it or not, the Nabisco Show took Southern gospel music out of Dixie and into homes in states as far away as Kansas and Nebraska. This attention paved the way for them to later appear on network shows with Arthur Godfrey, Tennessee Ernie Ford, Jimmy Dean, Peter Lind Hayes and others. They retired as winners on Godfrey's Talent Scouts show on CBS-TV. They did the music for Broadway shows and for Hollywood movies. They recorded for first Capitol then RCA Victor, following the Blackwood Brothers to the label.

Like the Melody Masters, the Blackwood Brothers had left the South, gone to the Midwest then returned. Into the 1950s, they were equally as powerful in the quartet world as the Statesmen.

When Wally Fowler would announce which groups would be appearing at one of his all-night singings, he was careful to note that either or both of these groups would be there. One of them would usually close the show.

In 1952, in Birmingham, the two prime ministers—Hovie Lister and James Blackwood—got together and made an agreement that changed the lives of both groups.

Bill Lyles, standing at the left, and R.W. Blackwood, seated on the right, were killed in a tragic plane crash at the Chilton County Peach Festival in 1954. Other members were Dan Huskey, James Blackwood and Jack Marshall, bottom. They began a partnership with the Statesmen in 1952.

This window sign invited folks to the airport hanger for a week of activities at the Chilton County Peach Festival, highlighted by a big gospel music show.

They would travel together. They would sing together. One phone call could book them both. On weekends, other groups would join the lineup-often the Speer Family-but during the week, it was the Statesmen and the Blackwood Brothers or the Blackwood Brothers and the Statesmen— depending on which camp you were in.

"It was good business in the beginning. They had their fans and we had our fans. Bring them together and there was a house full. But it went beyond good business. We were friends. Pretty soon, we had buses alike and could communicate by two-way radios. We were booked together 75 percent of the time," James Blackwood says.

When the Statesmen sang in Tuscaloosa, Alabama, the show was sponsored by the local Shrine Club and the Shriners got up and clapped during a rousing spiritual.

They became competitive partners. They still tried to get the best spot for their record table. They still mentally tabulated who sold the most. They still had an applause meter in their head that gauged who the crowd was enjoying.

There was also an apparent rivalry between the two lead singers—Blackwood and Jake. Fans talked about it. Other groups compared the two. Today, when younger singers talk about their influences, they talk about that pair. Blackwood says it was never an issue between the two of them.

"All those years I never felt it was a rivalry. We have been friends, buddies. When he hit a home run, I said, hooray for Jake, hooray for the Lord. There has never a jealous point in all those years," Blackwood says.

The Statesmen-Blackwoods union produced success, but it also produced sorrow, sorrow that touched the lives of both groups and of people who listened to their music.

Like the others who were there, Jake gives a detailed play-by-play of a night in Clanton, Alabama, when the two groups had gathered for a singing that was the end of a festive week in that community.

It was early in the evening of June 30, 1954, at the airport hangar where the show would be held. Jake and Bill Lyles of the Blackwoods were putting up their records when R.W. Blackwood came up and asked Lyles to come with him, saying he wanted to test the runway.

The Blackwoods had started flying to many of their dates and R.W. was the pilot. He was going to take off and land, so he would be comfortable with the air strip that night. Lyles didn't want to go, but R.W. insisted. When they got to the plane, John Ogburn, the son of the local promoter, just back from the Army, asked if he could go along.

"I went back and changed clothes but when I heard the plane taking off I wandered out there with everybody else.

*Hovie Lister always loved politics. The year the Statesmen
began was also the year Herman Talmadge was elected
governor of Georgia. They became friends and Talmadge
made the quartet singing ambassadors. The group often
sang at state functions at the governor's mansion in Atlanta.*

There was a crowd, maybe a thousand people and R.W. was
putting on a show for them. He made two attempts at the field
and on the second one, he bounced, which I had seen him do
before. Then, as far as I'm concerned, he froze to the stick. It
hit on an engine and a wing and just like that went up in
flames," Jake describes.

Panic took over. Jake saw James Blackwood, a frantic
expression on his face, staring into the blaze. He thought he saw
something. He thought it was his brother and he began to run
toward the plane.

"I just grabbed and bear-hugged him. My legs were black and blue for weeks where he kicked at me, trying to get loose. I had all my heart and I was pretty strong back then. I didn't put him down until he was all right," Jake says.

All three passengers in the plane were dead. For everyone who was there, it was a nightmare. James asked Jake to call the family back in Memphis, so they wouldn't hear it on radio.

The Blackwoods had lost a brother. The Statesmen had lost a member of their extended family. A few days later, crowded into the Ellis Auditorium, the Statesmen sang at R.W.'s funeral, a service that would not be equaled in that city until the burial of Elvis Presley, who as a young man was in the audience that afternoon.

"As far I'm concerned, to this day, R.W. Blackwood is still the best singer that's ever been in gospel music. He was our first soul singer. He could sing high and he could sing low. He had so much more to offer," Jake says.

Understandably, that night was a blur for James Blackwood. It was many years before he learned that the man who kept him out of that fire was his fellow lead singer, Jake Hess.

"He saved my life," Blackwood says.

The Statesmen put him in a Cadillac they were driving and took him back to Memphis. In the car, he vowed never to sing again.

Jake kept insisting he would, but Blackwood said no. As he began to realize that life had to go on, he asked who would replace Lyles, who would sing bass?

"J.D. Sumner," Jake said.

He did join the Blackwoods, and once again they were on the road together, a little older but still with a streak of mischief in them.

When they checked into hotels, they serenaded the woman behind the desk while James Blackwood cringed. When they were selling songbooks, they took shots at each other while James Blackwood blushed.

Many nights, they would be in an auditorium that also housed the school band. If Sumner was on stage, Jake might clang a cymbal. If Jake was on stage, Sumner might beat a bass drum.

They were in Mississippi one night when Jake played a trick on Sumner during a solo and as the Blackwoods left the stage he asked Lister to be sure that Jake did a number early in their stand.

Sneaking around backstage, Sumner found a tuba. Jake was singing, "If God Didn't Care" and as he got to the end of the number, Sumner emerged and blew into the instrument. He knew nothing about playing it, but he did it anyway. Somehow, he played a note. It blended perfectly with the last note of the song.

The audience demanded an encore. Jake hit his note but Sumner, to his chagrin, never could make that tuba do anything.

Their exchanges carried over to record sales. The two of them were in charge of the group's labels and when they got to a town, they would make the rounds of record stores.

"You don't want to buy those records," Jake would tell the store owner. "They have this tall bass singer who growls into the microphone."

"Now, I don't want to tell you how to do your business," Sumner would say, pointing to a stack of Statesmen records, "but those records won't sell. Their lead singer sings with his hands instead of his voice."

Joining the groups together was a major move in gospel music. New people heard the music. New people bought tickets

Tennessee Ernie Ford was once a DJ on WGST in Atlanta so he was well acquainted with Southern gospel music. He showed his love for the music by recording a number of popular sacred albums and by having the Statesmen as guests on his network television show.

in the auditorium. These 10 men learned from one another and they played off of each other. It was an important time for both groups.

They were the masters of the stage and out in the audience people were watching and listening, wondering what it would be like if they were on that stage.

Jim Wesson of the Chuck Wagon Gang was one.

"I was a 12-year-old boy and my folks took me to the Battle of the Songs in Fort Worth, the Statesmen and the Blackwoods. My parents had been going and I had no idea what it was about. I'll never forget it. No other singer had ever gripped me like Jake Hess did that night. I was mesmerized, to watch them work as a team, to hear him craft a song. Jake became my idol and from then on, there was nothing I wanted to be other than a lead singer like him," Wesson says.

Tim Lovelace of the Florida Boys stood shyly by the record tables.

"My parents had all the Statesmen records. Their record player could make them sound like the Chipmunks. While my folks would be gone, I'd stand there and play Jake. Finally, I got to see him at the Creighton Church of God in Mobile. I was 6, with freckles and big ears. I looked like Howdy Doody. We went in and there he was, my absolute hero. He must have seen me looking up at him so he came over. Jake told my daddy what a fine boy I was. He patted me on the head and messed up my hair and I couldn't say a thing. When he walked away, I told my parents that I wanted to be in a group. I wanted to be like Jake," Lovelace says.

Mark Trammell of Gold City was in Little Rock.

"When I was 4 years old I heard the Statesmen sing. I was living in Little Rock and they came to the Robinson Auditorium. I will never forget it. I knew right then what I wanted to do with my life."

Jake Hess can understand what people like them felt. When he was a child, he watched the groups that came through Haleyville. He traveled with his brothers to Montgomery to hear the Speers and had the first spaghetti he had ever tasted at their house, sitting across from Rosa Nell, one of the family's singing daughters. He had a dream and this was it.

No one thought the dream would end, but there were heartaches ahead, serious enough to change lives and careers.

On March 21, 1957, Denver Crumpler died at his home in Atlanta while the rest of the group was getting ready to load

Rosie Rozell brought new energy to the stage when he joined the Statesmen in 1958.

Jerry Lee Lewis could have been a rousing gospel piano player if he hadn't gone into rock 'n' roll. Throughout his early career, he was managed by Jud Phillips who was manager of the Daniel Quartet, when Jake was with them. Several times Lewis stopped by auditoriums to visit with the Statesmen.

the bus for a swing through Mississippi. It was a blow, for though he was not around during its creation, his classy style had come to personify what the Statesmen stood for.

Crumpler's loss hit the gospel industry hard.

"He was a pro. Some tenors didn't like to hit high notes early in the morning. They'd ask you to go down a step. Not Denver. He just loved to sing. When any of us wanted to break on stage, Hovie could always call on Denver for a solo. He loved it and so did the crowd," Jake says.

Thus ended what some observers have called "the perfect quartet." For Hovie, Jake, Chief and Doy, it was sad, but after paying their respects to Crumpler's family, it was time to sing again.

After Crumpler's death, Cat Freeman returned to the Statesmen—again. He soon began to blend in with the sound and with them singing so often with the Blackwoods, he began to taunt and pester J.D. Sumner. Their ad-libs and their standard stage routines are still remembered. So are his exchanges with Lister who took advantage of Freeman's non-stop humor.

Freeman stayed with the group until late 1958. As he often did, Freeman decided to move on and Rosie Rozell, a former Tulsa, Oklahoma, police officer became the Statesmen's tenor.

It was a departure from the tone of a Crumpler, but Rozell brought a new dimension to the group with a Pentecostal style that appealed to an entirely different audience. His rendition of "Oh, What a Savior," would become a gospel classic.

Bill Gaither was an aspiring songwriter at the time. He had been hearing the group sing since the early 1950s when his father took him to the Ryman Auditorium from their home in Indiana. Now an established leader in the gospel music field, he has rekindled his love of quartet music through his successful video series. Looking back at the transition between Crumpler and Rozell, he talks about how it changed the group's musical focus.

"The thing I have found out about groups is that when you lose one person you gain with the other."

Denver was the classic Irish tenor, very humble yet classy, a gentleman. Enter Rosie. He brought a thing Denver never had. Denver could never have done. 'Hide Thou Me.' Rosie did. He came from another background, a Pentecostal background. So he added a fire that they would never have had with Denver," Gaither says.

Behind the scenes, the Statesmen had become an empire. No one thought this could be threatened but Jake Hess says he began to feel they were growing complacent. They were mainly singing songs published by their company, often written by each other. The old spark was getting dull.

In the beginning, they sang a lot of Mosie Lister numbers, but they freely sang from other songwriter's books. On stage, they had always relied on instinct as well as experience. If Jake jumped on the bench, Hovie jumped higher. If Chief went to the audience, Jake followed. They rehearsed but they also were creative. Often, they used that same instinct when it came time to select new songs. No more. Now they looked into one catalogue—their own.

He talked to Lister, especially about the material, suggesting that they might have been passing up some good new material.

"Hovie said, look at your SESAC check," he says, meaning the royalty checks he was cashing. "And it would have been difficult for anyone to look at another person in the group and say he thought we could find a better piece of material somewhere else. You would be taking money away from your friend."

This was a throwback to the days of Vaughan and Stamps-Baxter groups who were locked into the songbooks they were selling. Jake remembered meeting Glenn Payne of the Cathedrals when he was singing with the Stamps Quartet.

Payne also remembers.

"We were in Birmingham. Jake was with the Melody Masters and they blew us away that night. They could sing anything and we were singing our songs. Everybody knew our songs but what they were doing seemed fresh and new," Payne says.

Now, in the early 1960s, Jake wanted what he was doing to be fresh and new. He didn't want to be satisfied. He wanted to be proud.

He remembered his goal as a young boy. He had wanted to sing in America's number one gospel quartet and it wasn't vanity that made him know that since 1948—particularly from 1957 to 1962—he had been singing lead for a group that everyone would remember as legends.

Another early goal of his had been to lead his own group, a group that just sang. He had heard a woman in the audience tell a newcomer not to applaud because if she did the group would keep singing the same song. He wanted one that stood there with their feet on the stage and sang. No encores. No gimmicks. Just sing.

He confided in Armond Morales of the Weatherfords whom he wanted to sing bass. He talked to Henry Slaughter who was music director at the Cathedral of Tomorrow with Rex Humbard about playing piano. He wanted Sherrill Nielson of the Speer Family to be the tenor. Finally, after they all mulled over candidates for baritone, he remembered Gary McSpadden, a preacher's kid in Lubbock, Texas, who had filled in for him with the Statesmen while he was hospitalized with a kidney problem.

Then, on a plane trip to New York, he told Hovie Lister, confirming the gossip he had already heard. They were at 20,000 feet when he told him.

"I told him I would be leaving by the end of the year. I don't think he believed it until he heard it from me," Jake says.

Gospel quartets usually considered a singer "dead" once he gave notice. The Statesmen had operated that way before. When Bobby Strickland said he was leaving there was an emergency tenor on stage that very night in 1949. Hovie Lister didn't handle Jake's decision that way. They were too close for that.

When word spread, gospel music people were shocked. You did not leave the Statesmen. But Jake was leaving, and nobody understood, least of all the loyal fans of the group and of Jake.

After the Statesmen won on Arthur Godfrey's Talent Scouts, they were invited to be part of his daily morning show on CBS-TV. The McGuire Sisters were regulars on the show and they appreciated the harmonies of this quartet from Georgia.

"I cried," says Mickey Vaughn. Still, an avid Jake Hess follower, she was a teenager and she had been upset enough one night a year before when she had gone into the Will Rogers Auditorium in Fort Worth and McSpadden was standing in Jake's spot.

"People like me thought we'd never see Jake again. We didn't want anybody singing his songs."

Lister decided that Jack Toney, would be in the group's new lead singer. He had been singing with the Dixie Echoes and, like the man he was replacing, was a native of North Alabama. Within a few weeks he was traveling with quartet, learning his parts and getting comfortable with the fellows he would be singing around.

Toney, tall and talented, was soon singing the Statesmen's greatest hits. Jake had sensed the group needed a change in material, but Toney sang out of the same book.

"Jack was and is a great singer, one of the greatest lead singers who has ever been in our business. But think how much greater he would have been with great songs of his own to sing," Jake says.

Jim Hill is another who followed Jake in the Statesmen. He says he had to deal with those who remembered it the way it was.

"I made a decision—right or wrong—that I was going to be me," Hill says. "I couldn't be anyone else."

Buddy Burton sang baritone with a 1995 edition of the Statesmen and Toney again sang lead. A few years ago, Burton stood in that spot. He said people looked back at the Statesmen of the Jake Hess era as nostalgic.

"They were the real thing. If you have a counterfeit, there must have been a original and they were the originals," Burton says.

Burton looks back at that original group as a team.

"Jake says there wouldn't have been a Jake Hess without a Hovie Lister but I don't think there would have been a Hovie without a Jake. He was as much at the top of his field as Hovie was at his," Burton says.

Lister knew there were comparisons.

"All we asked was that people accept the new sound. We still want that today," Lister says.

Jake Hess sang his final note with the original Statesmen on December 7, 1963, in Chicago. An important era in gospel music ended at Medina Hall.

"Hovie said something about it that night from the stage. He gave me a send-off and I appreciated that," Jake says.

By the time Jake prepared to leave the Statesmen even the fun they had on stage couldn't overshadow the dream he was about to fulfill with the Imperials.

Jake Hess got on an airplane and Jack Toney got on the bus with the Statesmen. Jake was alone.

A new group would be coming to his house that week to begin work. But that night, he was alone. He had been through a lot with those guys he was leaving. They were closer to him than the brothers he had been born with. He was alone, but now he realizes that in so many ways, they have never really parted.

"I know that when I die, I will be a Statesman."

JAKE HESS AND THE IMPERIALS

7

A Healing in Winston-Salem

The other four were just short of being cocky but there was nothing short about Jake Hess. He was cocky. He knew the fellows he had surrounded himself with could sing. For nearly two years they had been proving that, on records and on stages. They could sing all right. No show business. No funny stuff. Just sing. But when promoters had been putting together the concerts in the major auditoriums, his group had been dressed up with no place to sing.

Which led them to Winston-Salem, North Carolina, in 1965. They were the Imperials. A lot of suggestions had been

The original Imperials were Sherrill Nielson, Henry Slaughter, Jake, Gary McSpadden and Armond Morales. They were a handpicked group, recruited from other quartets. From the beginning, they had a policy that they would never repeat a song if they did an encore.

kicked around before Jake Hess secured the rights to that name from Marion Snider, the talented keyboard player for the Imperial Sugar Quartet, a popular group in Texas. Jake knew the importance of the right name. He wanted something original. He wanted something that fit, and Imperials seemed to fit this hand-picked lineup.

They had come to Atlanta to Jake's house in December of 1963 ready to work. By then, nothing about what they were doing was secret. Record executives were calling every day, wanting to know what was happening. Some even came to see for themselves. Excitement was high.

Henry Slaughter arrived with 35 or 40 arrangements already worked out. For months, he had been working diligently, keeping in mind the individual voices who would be singing these songs, even though the five of them hadn't even been in the same room together.

"I could hear them sing in my mind and I wrote with those four voices in mind. I was inspired. I had never been in a group before where there was not a weak spot—not a one," Slaughter says.

When they finally heard themselves together they knew this was a special sound. Different, but special. Armond Morales was smooth, not growling like so many other bass singers. Sherrill Nielson, the youngest member of the group, wasn't a screaming tenor. Gary McSpadden had no rough edges and could take a lead as well as blend. Henry Slaughter was the creator, at the keyboard, as the arranger and as the emcee.

"THE IMPERIAL SUGAR QUARTET"

Left to right:
Floyd Gray
    Bass
Jake Baumgardner
    Baritone
Homer Tankersley, Jr.
    Second Tenor
Charles Speed
    First Tenor
At the Piano:
Marion Snider

FRESHER BECAUSE IT'S THE ONLY SUGAR REFINED IN TEXAS
Tune in Monday, Wednesday, and Friday

Dallas, WFAA-820 11:45am-12:00 Noon
Amarillo, KGNC 11:45am-12:00 Noon
Texarkana, KCMC 9:45am-10:00am
San Antonio, WOAI 11:45am-12:00 Noon
Houston, KPRC 11:45am-12:00 Noon

Marion Snider gave permission to use the name Imperials.

"As for Jake, he was a pacesetter, a singer with his own identity. I've heard orchestra leaders call a person 'a singer's singer.' Jake was that. He could do anything a composer or arranger wanted him to do," Slaughter says.

Their material was tooled to fit their style, individually and collectively. They could sing the traditional quartet music that people loved and expected. But the Imperials wanted more. They were putting together a song list that would include the new with the old.

Given all of this, they still hadn't had a chance to sing their songs on the major stages. Winston-Salem was the place where to a man the Imperials decided they would sing—whether the other groups sang or not.

For months, the Imperials had been getting cancellation calls from promoters. Some of them sent a check. Most just sent an apology. Twice that had happened in Winston-Salem.

They suspected it might happen again and when the phone call from promoter C.R. McClain came, Jake was ready for him.

"Twice he had sent us checks to stay home. When he called to say he was going to have to do that again, I told him no, we were going to sing. When he said the other groups wouldn't sing with us, I said, fine, we will be the five fellows in the audience, dressed alike and telling the folks why we aren't up there singing," Jake says.

Brock Speer, after hearing the Imperials in a recording session, had warned Jake that this group might not be accepted. "Maybe they're too good," Speer had said. But the obstacle to the Imperials singing wasn't how good they were.

Promoters in these major cities had feared some of the big name groups might not sing if the Imperials were there so they had been turning away Jake's group.

The Imperials could sing old-fashioned gospel songs or some of the newer sounds. They are seen today as a transitional group between the past and contemporary Christian music.

It wasn't personal. It was business. And it was business that brought the Imperials to Winston-Salem that night. They got there early and set up their record table in the lobby. Anyone who saw them would have thought it was business as usual.

In Jake's coat pocket were the canceled checks for the other shows in that building where they had been paid not to sing. If it came down to it, he would present those checks as evidence to anyone who wanted to see them. He knew that the other fellows agreed with him that it was time for this to end.

Backstage, McLain pleaded with them.

"Some quartets say if you sing they won't sing. Do you think you guys can do two hours?" the promoter asked.

"And never repeat a song," Jake said.

The Imperials sang that night in Winston-Salem and so did all of the other groups who were booked. The ice was broken at last.

"There was never any anger about this on either side. Not an ugly word was spoken. All of it was over business. Now, over the years, there has been a lot of healing. The Lord does that, doesn't He?" Jake says.

The Imperials were a group that broke ice in other ways. They had been created from established groups, something Mom Speer warned Jake about. "Your sins will come back to you," she said, upset that he was taking away Nielsen, their promising tenor.

For Nielson, not yet 20, there was pressure from every direction. Jake wanted him. Brock and Ben Speer were asking him to stay with them, promising they soon would be going to an all-male group. Then, from out of nowhere, Hovie Lister called and said he wanted him to replace Jake in the Statesmen.

"These were people that not long before I had only dreamed of just meeting. I thought I had died and gone to heaven. But the Imperials were new, I had a chance to establish myself as me. I'm proud I did," Nielsen says.

There was another difference that the public did not know about. It was not an indictment of the other groups. It was simply something Jake thought was appropriate since the Imperials were gospel singers. It was new in 1963, but today is commonplace in the industry.

The Imperials, as part of their contract, had to sign a morals clause that stipulated if they were guilty of a break in morals they would be fired. The clause spelled out what things were considered violations. Jake even added a twist that an offending individual would have to tell his wife and family why he was fired.

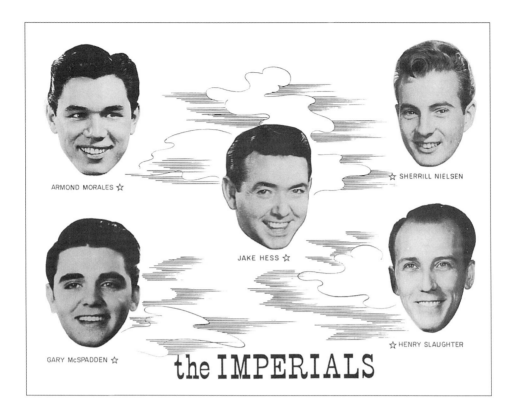

ARMOND MORALES ☆

☆ SHERRILL NIELSEN

JAKE HESS ☆

☆ HENRY SLAUGHTER

GARY McSPADDEN ☆

the IMPERIALS

This clause was important to Jake.

"I've never been too good at judging people. We should leave that to the Lord. Among quartet people, as long as they took care of their job, as long as they were not bringing a problem on to the stage, it was none of my business. Yet it was. It would give me an ache inside. When I would see something like that, I wanted to say, 'You dirty dog, you're not fit to be singing gospel music.' But I wasn't comfortable doing that with other people. With my own group, I wanted to take care of those things," Jake says.

McSpadden remembers the day that was discussed.

"It is normal today for this to be in a contract with a record label or an agency. When the group first talked about

For nearly two years, the Imperials had to keep their bags packed for they went all over the country since major promoters in the South refused to put the group on stage.

it, we said we wanted guys who loved the Lord and weren't just shamming this whole thing. Not that many people did, but there had been people who did. I know not everybody is out here to minister. In the old days, not all of them were Christians. They just sang the music. We decided that gospel musicians and gospel music touches lives. There is a message to be delivered. You can't do that if your own life isn't in order," McSpadden says.

There were other rules to be set, though they paled in comparison. And since Jake was the leader of the group, he was the one who policed the others. One of the things he always insisted on was punctuality. This was part of his traditional concept of what constituted a Quartet Man. You always put the group first.

"He wanted to be tough, but his bark was always worse than his bite. But he really was a stickler about being on time. He always told us that if you're late for the bus, bring your car. You won't be riding on the bus. Then one morning, we were all there. Except Jake. We drove to his house. I was the one who got to go to the door and wake him up," Nielsen laughs.

They also wanted to break new ground musically, which Slaughter believes they were able to accomplish in several ways.

"We wanted to widen the scope of gospel music and take off the lid. Before, you had been limited. This meant you appealed only to a certain group of people. We wanted to expand and we did. Some of the diehards wanted us to be like everyone else. But they came to respect that we were different," Slaughter says.

These were things that a little more than a decade before people had said about the Statesmen. They had broken all of the old rules and established a new set of standards that others soon were following.

In the 1960s, it was the Imperials. No one knew it at the time, but they were building a bridge between the traditional sound and what has come to be known as contemporary Christian music. Today, that genre of music has been labeled as the fastest growing art form in American music by the New York Times. For the Imperials, that transition was at times controversial though to Jake it was nothing new.

"We waited a while before we started changing the instrumentation on stage. Until then, Henry's piano had been an 88-key orchestra. Then we added drums, guitar and bass. People didn't like it. 'You're ruining the whole thing,' they thought. We were also blasted by other groups, but pretty soon they had them, too. Music was changing and so were we. Most of this was Jake's idea and we jumped in the boat with him and said 'Let's row together,'" McSpadden says.

The first time that the curtain raised and, on cue, the Imperials band began to play, everyone in the auditorium noticed. A few groups had had guitars over the years, but these were electric. It was like the night someone first plugged in the instruments on the Grand Ole Opry. And there were only guitars out there. The Imperials had drums.

A scattered few got up and left. But the young people who were there realized that someone was playing their music at last. Barriers were being broken that would never again be rebuilt. Soon the Imperials were being booked on college campuses, something that hadn't happened before.

Again, it was a throwback to the Statesmen which had been roundly attacked for those sinful horns that showed up on some of their records and for their "hoochie-koochie" manner on stage.

After getting started in Atlanta, the Imperials and Jake soon found it would be more convenient if they moved to Nashville. They had been spending a lot of time on the bus traveling since their syndicated television show was taped there. It seemed to be the thing to do, but a few months after each one of them moved in, the show was canceled. They still hoped to do session work, but this was a town full of would-be backup singers. Why would anyone hire a new group in a new town?

RCA Victor did. Thanks to Mary Lynch. She was secretary to Chet Atkins and later would marry Felton Jarvis, Elvis Presley's record producer. She had also been president of the Statesmen Fan Club so she knew Jake Hess and what he stood for.

"I hired all the backup singers for RCA and I knew Elvis was coming to town to record. Elvis just idolized Jake. He was

When the curtain went up and the Imperials band started to play it was more than an 88-key orchestra. Band members were Dave Mathews on guitar, Larry Benson on drums and Joe Moscheo on piano. Quartet members were Gary McSpadden, Jim Murray, Armond Morales and Jake Hess.

his favorite all-time singer. Felton produced Elvis and he told him there was a new group in town that he'd like to try on background. Elvis asked him who it was and when Felton said Jake Hess was singing lead, he said, 'Get him. Get him. Get him.' So Elvis used the Imperials on 'How Great Thou Art," which was a Grammy Award album," said Mary Lynch Jarvis, in a conversation before she died in the summer of 1995.

The Imperials, in four short years, had accomplished so much. They were begrudgingly acclaimed among their peers in gospel music and in other areas of the music world. Like the Statesmen, people still talk about that generation of Imperials in

Jim Murray, left, replaced Sherrill Nielsen, joining Gary McSpadden, Jake, Armond Morales and Henry Slaughter. This still was from the movie, "Sing Me a Song for Heaven's Sake."

awe. Jake Hess could mark one more goal off his list. He had had his own group and they could go out on a stage and—flat-footed as he always puts it—sing, really sing.

Only standing there and singing had become a problem for Jake Hess himself. For the first part of his life, until nephritis declared war on his kidneys in 1962, he had been embarrassingly healthy.

His kidney problems arose after they started talking about the Imperials. He was still with the Statesmen and the others were still singing with their respective groups. Jake wondered if they should go through with their plan so he called Morales.

"Armond, I may have to rethink our decision. I don't know if I'll be able," he said.

Armond Morales told Jake something that lingers with him today. He thinks about it whenever he wonders if he will be able to face an obstacle.

"Don't limit God," Morales said.

Soon, the disease was under control, but nephritis, or Bright's disease, never goes away so years later, when he was with the Imperials, he was still going to the doctor for frequent checkups. This time it wasn't his kidneys. This time it was his heart.

"Get off the road or you'll have a heart attack," he was warned. It was the first time anyone had been so blunt but it would not be the last.

The Imperials became a popular backup group on Nashville recording sessions—thanks to Jake's old friend, Mary Lynch. They sang on Elvis Presley's first Grammy-winning album.

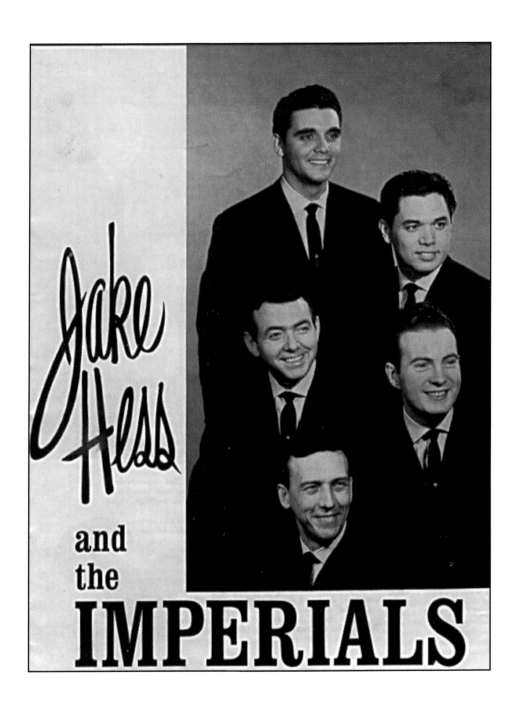

He had been a regular part of the Eddie Hill Show, a popular television program on Nashville's WLAC-TV. The station had told him there was more work there if he wanted it. It wouldn't be the life he had always dreamed about, but he would still be singing.

Now he had to tell the quartet.

This wouldn't be easy, he knew. This was his group, and the fellows in it had taken this chance because he asked them to. As for Jake, he didn't know if he'd ever sing in a quartet again.

The Imperials were in Kentucky for an electrical co-op convention. Most of the guys were out wandering around but Jake was talking with Ron Ham, their guitar player. Ham was

Jake always wanted a group that could stand flat-footed and sing. The Imperials did just that. This lineup was Jim Murray, Jake, Gary McSpadden, Armond Morales and Henry Slaughter.

sharing some personal troubles and telling Jake that he might be leaving. Jake told him what he had been having trouble putting into words.

Back on the bus, he was alone with McSpadden who couldn't believe all that had happened to him those last few years. As a kid, he had been drawn to Jake who had befriended him and inspired him. When he had kidney problems, Jake insisted that the Statesmen let this unknown college kid sing in his place. Jake had become his big brother. Then came the Imperials, which led them to that bus.

"Gooey, I've got something to tell you," said Jake, who had started calling him that when his youngest son couldn't say Gary.

"I've got something to tell you, too," McSpadden said.

Neither remembers who went first, but they found that each of them was preparing to leave the group. Jake for his health. McSpadden because being on the road was threatening his family.

The Imperials would go on. Armond Morales is still on the road singing with the group today. But in 1967, the group was changing. First Slaughter, then McSpadden and Hess. They left behind a legacy of change in an industry that often treats change like a deadly disease.

"We weren't striving to be different. We just went as far as you could go in the contemporary direction and stay in Southern gospel music," Jake says.

Still, he looks back at the group like a critic—not of the Imperials, but of himself.

"I don't think I was qualified from a business standpoint. Had I been a Hovie Lister, a good businessman, there would have been no limits to what we could have done. We did well, but we never did move to that next level. I had the ideas, but I

The Music City Singers appeared with Jake on his TV show in Nashville. They were Woody Beatie, his wife Peggy and Ed Enoch. Beatie is now the keyboard player for the Palmetto State Quartet and Enoch sings lead with the Stamps Quartet.

follow better than I lead. On that side of it, being able to sing is the least of it," he says.

And before Jake left the Imperials there was other business to be considered. He had founded this group in his own home. He recruited the other fellows. He had poured most of his personal savings into getting the group started. By then, there was also a booking agency that had spun off the Imperials.

A deal was worked out where Jake would get the agency and an ongoing 15 percent from The Imperials. Once the lawyers and accountants were through with the deal, it was costing him $300 just to leave. He figured that there would always be that 15 percent.

But in less than a month, two members of the group came to see him and explained that like him they had put everything they had into the group. "You just had more," they said. They told him that he wouldn't be getting that 15 percent.

Then and now, Jake Hess harbors no bitterness. Only surprise at how God has blessed him, or, as the song he often sings puts it: how God has taken real good care of him.

"It amazes me. I've never gone without a job. Every time I get to that place, I have two or three things to do. I never prepared myself to do anything else but sing gospel music. I studied the shaped notes. I studied harmony and voice. I finished high school on the road. I am qualified to sing in a quartet and nothing else. The rest of the things I have tried in life, I was never prepared for," he says.

Yet, overnight, Jake became a television personality. The station expanded his role on the Eddie Hill Show and began using him in other ways. He was off the road for the first time since he was 15 years old. Things were going well, however. The television audience was enjoying him, even if he believed he could do nothing but sing.

But he still had that heart attack.

"I got to the station at 5 o'clock that morning and I went to Jimmy Norton, the director, and said something was wrong with me. He called Dr. Milton Grossman who said I was having a heart attack and for me to lie down," Jake says.

When Norton went to Jake to tell him what the doctor said, he couldn't find him. He had slipped out a side door and

The nucleus of the Sound of Youth were all named Hess. Starting with Jake, right, his oldest son Chris and his daughter Becky.

was in his car on the way to St. Thomas Hospital, swerving his way down the road. By the time he got there, his arm was numb. He went in the first door he could find, which proved to be the wrong one.

"You'll have to go around," a nurse said.

"I can't go anymore or anywhere," Jake said.

She put him in a wheelchair and pushed him into the emergency room where she found they were expecting him. "I don't know where he came from, but I got him out of the parking lot and he's clean," she said. They rushed him into the cardiac care unit where he looked better than most patients having a heart attack since he already had on his TV makeup.

Jake Hess won four Grammy Awards and also sang on a Grammy Award-winning album by Elvis Presley. His first came for this album: "Everything Is Beautiful."

It was serious. Doctors didn't think he would survive. Soon, J.D. Sumner came by to see how his friend was doing. The physician was blunt.

"I wish I knew. He's bad. He's damn bad. We have done all we can do. It is up to Him," he said, pointing his finger toward the sky.

That doctor was only the first of many who underestimated both Jake and the God he served. There would be others who couldn't explain his ability to survive. In a few weeks, he was back at Channel 5.

"That was the day they fired me," Jake says.

Officials at the station didn't think a man who had suffered a heart attack could stand the rigors of a daily TV show. That day, it was mentioned on the air that he wouldn't be back and the station was flooded with calls from Jake's fans who demanded that he be put pack on the program.

He was.

By late that day, he had his job back. He would stay at WLAC-TV the next eight years, not counting that day he was unemployed.

After Eddie Hill retired because of health, the station gave Jake his own show. Temporarily of course. Eventually, he would do 12 shows a week. His ratings would make his noon show the highest rated local show in Nashville television. But through most of those years, he had to put up with David Reece.

That could be a chore, for the one-time keyboard player for the Rangers was the most unpredictable character that ever came on to a stage with Jake—even more outrageous than J.D. Sumner. Reece played piano with the combo that performed on Jake's show, but he went far beyond the piano.

There were the days he put his left shoe on his right foot and limped on to the set. There was the day he turned his face away from Jake and the camera so he could unveil that he had shaved off half of his mustache. There was the day he told Jake that he and his wife were expecting the patter of little feet at their house.

"My mother-in-law is coming and she's a midget," Reece joked.

As the popularity of the television show grew, so did Jake's fame around Nashville. He was in demand. He even became a regular at Vanderbilt University basketball games where he often sang the National Anthem.

Because he did that, he added a tape of The Star Spangled Banner to his box of tracks. That was a mistake as he learned one night in a small Kentucky town where he was singing in a church.

The well-meaning fellow who was running sound for him was supposed to put in the tapes that Jake introduced on stage. It sounds easy, but that guy was having trouble.

Jake would introduce one song and another would come out of the tape player. Jake could hardly keep from laughing so he turned to his sound man and said "Surprise me. Play whatever you want to play and I'll sing it."

That was a mistake.

You guessed it. The fellow reached into the stack of tapes and either by accident or out of spite, he played the National Anthem.

Jake did what he said he would. He sang it.

"That was a cheap way to get a standing ovation, wasn't it?" Jake laughs.

The Music City Singers were the backup singers on his TV show and soon they were merged into a group that became the Music City Singers. They included Ed Enoch, now the lead singer with the Stamps Quartet and Woody Beatie, the piano player for the Palmetto State Quartet.

"I was singing with a hero. James Blackwood and Jake Hess were always my favorites. James had the power and Jake had the finesse. I wanted a little of both and there I was, a kid just out of the Army, having a chance to learn from Jake," Enoch says.

The group started taking jobs in the area then expanded. The TV station told Jake that the only stipulation they had was that he always remind his audience—wherever he was—that he worked for WLAC-TV. If they were outside the viewing area,

Becky, Chris and Jake recorded several albums as the Sound of Youth. For Jake, it was a rewarding time as a father but one that was questioned as a career move.

Jake didn't know why he should say that. They told him to say that Channel 5 was the home of Hee-Haw.

At his own home, Jake was getting to see his children grow up. For Joyce and him, this was a new experience. There had always been too many good-byes. Now he was there in Nashville with Joyce, Becky, Chris and Jake Jr. It was a happy time for him. Only like their father, Becky and Chris wanted to sing. He knew the pitfalls, but he also knew the rewards. He wanted to share with them his knowledge of both.

From his desire to be there for his children came Jake Hess and the Sound of Youth. Becky was 18 and Chris was 16. With them, he gathered around him a group of kids from Belmont University in Nashville.

He remembered when all he wanted to do was sing and he enjoyed seeing others who shared that desire, even if some of them were not blessed with the natural ability that comes from God, not just from desire. He was putting together a venture that would cause disappointments but one that at the same time may have been the most rewarding years of his musical career.

Once again, he was going where others hadn't. Southern gospel music had always meant four men with four blue suits and a piano. At the time, family groups were not the norm. Children were left on the bus or backstage, not put on the stage, unless it was to milk some applause.

Now here was a graduate of that old school, a man the industry once crowned "Mr. Gospel Music," and he was traveling around the country with a bunch of kids. A bunch of kids was always said with disgust.

"People didn't like us. They didn't like the fact that Daddy wasn't with a quartet and they didn't like those drums. And all we wanted was to do something for the Lord. Everywhere we went, some person was putting us down. It was a rough time in his career and in his life," says his daughter, Becky Buck.

Most established gospel groups wouldn't be on the stage with them. Major promoters would book free shows if the Sound of Youth was singing somewhere else in their area. One of them even made a disgusting crack that he hoped Jake had a heart attack on stage if he went through with a concert in his town.

Old friends turned their backs on him.

"Brock Speer said it was great to see all those kids on stage, that it was the greatest thing I had ever done. The others weren't so nice," Jake says.

"When Dad started traveling with us, as far as a career move, it was crazy. He had just won two or three Grammy Awards and he was traveling with kids. What he was doing was investing his life in Becky, me and those other young people. We had the opportunity to be with him. I didn't go to seminary. But I traveled with Jake Hess," says Chris, who has served as a minister of youth in first Tennessee and now in Georgia.

One of the up-and-coming groups that was on the scene in the late 1960s was the Bill Gaither Trio. While others were refusing to sing with this entourage of 13 young people, the Gaithers joined them for a swing through Texas. It was the first time the Hess children had met this man who one day would be their friend and would play an important role in their father's life.

Gaither explains the feeling others had about this.

"People always thought of Jake with a professional group then, there he was, on a different level with his kids. We are in a Christian field but there is jealousy. He had been a person who always had it his way. He was that good. Some people may have said they were tired of him always getting to the top. We are human beings. People were used to hearing him sing with four men ... four great men ... but Jake didn't care. He wanted to be with his kids, to do that for them. Fans and the public can be cruel though. We like you like this, but we don't like it like this," Gaither says, remembering the reactions from people in the industry he loves.

Those feeling were expressed in various ways. The most cruel expression came in Nashville in 1976 when Jake went into the office of a long-time colleague who offered an assessment that left a man they called a legend wondering if this career he had built so carefully was at an end.

Jake Hess Jr. doesn't create in music but in the outdoors as a landscape designer.

Jake Hess Jr. doesn't create in music but in the outdoors as a landscape designer.

"Jake, I'm going to tell you something. We all get to a point in life when we have to say: this is it. Face it. People don't want to hear you anymore. You have had it," the man said.

This was a friend, a man he had know for years, a man he had confidence in. Jake Hess had been singing gospel music most of his life. The shelves and the walls at his home and at his office were filled with honors and awards. But at that moment, he was shattered.

Maybe people didn't want to hear him or his music anymore. Denver Crumpler had been dead nearly 20 years. James Wetherington, the Chief, had died three years before in a hotel room at the National Quartet Convention. Maybe it was time to quit. Quartet people were ridiculing him for singing with a group of kids. Insecurities he had fought since he was picking cotton in other people's fields came rushing back.

Standing in the parking lot outside this colleague's office. Jake started to cry. Sonny Simmons, an old friend who operated a popular booking agency in town, walked up and asked what was wrong. Jake told him what had been said and the man invited him up to his office. In his office were representatives of fair boards from around the country. A man from South Dakota had heard about Jake and the kids. They sounded like a group people would want to hear, he said. By the time they parted that afternoon, the Sound of Youth had been booked solid for the upcoming season.

"God steps in when you don't expect Him," Jake says.

After eight years with WLAC-TV, Jake had an unexpected call from a television evangelist in California. Dr. Ken Conley wanted Jake and the group to sing on a Christian network out there. It seemed like an opportunity to apply what he was doing to a Christian operation.

They hadn't been out there long before a guest was booked for the show who had written a book that predicted the exact date when Jesus was coming back. Everyone else scoffed at the book. Not Conley. He became obsessed with the man's prediction. Soon, everybody but the Hess family had left the station. Jake, Becky and Chris were on salary and they collected only two paychecks before the television job crumbled. Soon they had lost everything they came with, including their bus.

Jake wasn't sure what was ahead. He had been hungry before, but when the Melody Masters picked those peaches it was just a bunch of fellows trying to get by. This time, his children were involved and he felt guilty.

Gary Hopkins, a promoter in the area called and asked him if they wanted to work a two-night job and, of course, they said yes. They needed to work and they needed to be paid.

Dr. Gene Scott, a well-known Bible teacher, was doing his television show that night. Scott had a style unlike any other, often smoking a cigar standing in the pulpit. Scott had worked for Oral Roberts and he had a following in the Los Angeles area, attracting thousands to his University Cathedral. His address was P.O. Box 1, which Scott like to brag about.

Jake and the kids sang for Scott's service those two nights. Jake was impressed and so was Scott. They would work together for the next four years.

Becky had gone back to Nashville but Jake and Chris stayed on. From 1977 until 1981—when they weren't chalking up frequent flyer points between California and Tennessee, they were seeing a side of Christian music Jake had never seen before.

It was while he was working for Scott that Jake had to apply for a passport and discovered for the first time that he had lived that long without an official, legal name.

Scott was taking Jake and Chris with him to Taiwan. Over there, they would celebrate Freedom Day, an event that would garner international attention. The fact that none of the party spoke Chinese seemed unimportant.

Soon after Scott's group arrived, according to the Chinese calendar, it was New Year's, which in Taiwan is a major holiday. They were split into small groups and were to have a formal dinner at the homes of some of Scott's local supporters. An interpreter would meet them at the home, they were assured.

Jake and Chris were sent by car with the promise that someone who spoke the language would meet them at the end of their journey. When they arrived at this beautiful Chinese home, there was not an interpreter in sight.

"We made our way the best we could but you can grin and grunt for just so long. It was embarrassing," Jake says. "We were about to be seated for dinner when this American walked in the door."

"Why, Jake Hess!" he exclaimed.

Jake didn't know him but this fellow thankfully knew Jake Hess. The man was a teacher from Lexington, Kentucky. He used to be a regular viewer of Jake's noon show in Nashville. And he also spoke fluent Chinese.

"He may have saved our lives. Because when he sat down the table with us he was able to say 'Eat that,' or 'Don't eat that, it'll kill you.' And we never did find out what happened to that interpreter," he says.

At the Freedom Day ceremony, Jake and Chris sang before an estimated 20,000 people—most of them unable to understand the message in words though they enjoyed the music. Dr. Bob Jones, founder of the university that bears his name in South Carolina, was there and so were two United States Senators. Each thought he was going to be the main speaker.

Dr. Gene Scott was the speaker, however.

"Doc was good to me. He paid me well. I got to be good friends with his father and in conversation said I would sing 'It's Not All Over' at his funeral. Years later, I did just that."

While he was back in California for the funeral, Scott asked Jake to come back and sing for him again. There was no way, he could do that. He had obligations in Nashville.

"Doc said I could fly out on Saturday, sing a song on Sunday morning and fly right back. He paid for everything, even if I bought a Coca-Cola," Jake says.

Still, when Jake Hess looks back at that time in his life, his happiest memory are those years he spent chaperoning and teaching those 18 young people.

It wasn't the music.

"Sometimes we were so bad that Dad would come backstage and cry," Chris says.

The fact that few others understand is not an issue. All of that is overshadowed by the fact that his children understand and appreciate a time in his career that has never earned him a Grammy or put him in someone's hall of fame.

Surely, it wasn't the money.

"Money has never been a factor to Dad. The Sound of Youth would go anywhere. He didn't care how big or how small the church was. We were way out in New Mexico, in the desert. It was a little old block building. I remember us saying, 'We drove all the way for this?' But the Lord was there that night

As a young person, in Tupelo, Mississippi, and Memphis, Tennessee, Elvis Presley was capti-vated by the energy Jake, Hovie and Chief had with the Statesmen.

8

'I Want Your Friendship'

lvis was coming. Waiting on him was a studio full of musicians along with the usual suspects that followed him wherever he went whether they were needed or not. Felton Jarvis was among those who waited. Like always, he had a stack of demo records waiting for the needle on the turntable to drop. From that stack of vinyl would come the songs they would record that day.

This was the way Elvis Presley operated. He left it up to Jarvis, his producer, to select the long list. Elvis took it from there, listening to the songs on the demos and like an emperor ruling whether a gladiator in the arena lived or died, he decided which songs would be on the album they were about to record.

The Jordanaires knew the routine so when Elvis started the familiar ritual they stood off to the side trying to appear interested. This wouldn't take long for Elvis often listened to only a few bars before deciding.

Jarvis was putting them on and taking them off when one of the demos made Gordon Stoker and the Jordanaires

When Elvis said Jake was his major influence, recording executives wanted him to leave gospel music.

stop and listen more closely.

"That's Jake," one of them said.

"Couldn't be, but it's someone doing a Jake Hess imitation," Gordon Stoker said.

Like the others, Stoker knew Jake's voice well. They were both alumni of the John Daniel Quartet, though that had been years ago. They had been working around Jake Hess for many years. They understood well what was happening.

"Somebody knew how much Elvis admired Jake Hess. They thought if their demo sounded like Jake, Elvis would stop and listen to it," Stoker says.

It worked.

Elvis asked Jarvis to play the song again. Then he motioned for Stoker and the Jordanaires to come closer.

"Can you guys do that?" he asked.

"All of us stood there and did our best Jake since that was what the demo was doing," Stoker says.

"That's what I want," Elvis said.

The song was "My Wish Came True" and Stoker says if you listen to the recording you will hear the Jordanaires in the background sounding a lot like Jake Hess.

Whoever put together that demo was aware what anyone who had done their homework on Elvis Presley already knew. When he became a private in the United States Army, in 1958, inquiring reporters asked who his musical influences were and on his list was the name of Jake Hess.

That sent the newsmen scurrying to find out who this Hess fellow was. More interested than the reporters were the record producers who wondered what was going to happen to pop music with the man someone would later crown the King of Rock 'n' Roll wearing Army green instead of blue suede shoes.

Finding out who Jake Hess was should have been easy for the gentlemen at RCA Victor, for like Elvis, Jake and the Statesmen Quartet had been recording for the label since 1954. It wasn't long before Jake's phone began to ring.

"People didn't know me from a sack of sand. They might have known about the Statesmen, but they didn't know me. But because Elvis said I was something special they wanted to be the first to bring me to New York," says Jake, who had already been to the Big Apple when the Statesmen were winners on Arthur Godfrey's Talent Scouts four years earlier.

People in gospel music already knew that Presley admired Jake Hess and loved the music he sang. He had always hung around the auditoriums when the Statesmen, the Blackwood Brothers and other groups came to Tupelo, Mississippi, where he was born and to Memphis, Tennessee, where he moved as a teenager.

"We knew Elvis before he was Elvis," Jake says, remembering this earnest young man who had an endless number of questions for whoever would take the time to talk to him.

All of this was new to the people who began to call Jake. They had a plan. They had even contacted someone at Styles Unlimited in New York who would take care of the hairpiece he already was wearing.

"I was going to be a 'star,' or so they said. They were talking fast. But see, someone like me, they couldn't understand. I was already making enough money, more that I ever dreamed I'd make in my life. We had a record company. We were making as many dates as we could fill. I was doing all right," he says.

These were not people whose vocabulary included the word "no." They were dangling a lot of promises in front of this gospel singer Elvis liked. They thought he would be awed. Instead, he was reluctant to even talk to them when they called.

Bud Prager got involved. As president of SESAC, he had worked with Jake Hess on the Statesmen publishing company, educating him about the pitfalls of copyright laws.

"He kept me out of jail," Jake laughs.

They met through SESAC, a music licensing organization. Hess, with his Alabama roots, had to enlist the help of this New York executive.

"He was coming to Atlanta and we would be expected to entertain this New York sharpie. I heard he liked barbecued chicken so we grilled up several of them. He liked them all right. He ate enough to make himself sick," Jake says.

As they were clearing the table, Joyce asked him if he wanted any dessert.

"What do you have?" he asked her.

"Nothing," Joyce said, "I just figured it was safe to ask somebody who had eaten as much as you did."

J.D. Sumner and the Blackwoods sang at Elvis' mother's funeral. Later, he put together the group that sang at Presley's funeral.

A friendship began that night, but Prager says it wasn't friendship that made him think a pop music career was a real possibility for Jake.

"Jake is a stylist. You can hear that he's not a regular singer. He's also a bright guy with a lot of gifts and a lot of talents. Some of the great singers don't know how to make themselves greater. He did," says Prager, who for 17 years managed the rock group "Foreigner."

Michael Guido also got involved. He was a minister Jake had met when he conducted a revival service at Jake's church in Decatur, Georgia. They had become friends and when these offers were dropped on the table, Jake called Guido and asked him to hurry to Atlanta.

"It was a real struggle. I think Jake wanted me to tell him what to do, what God would want him to do. All I suggested was that he pray over his decision," Guido says.

"If I had known he was praying with that guy and that was going to make the difference I would have come down to Atlanta and out-prayed them," Prager laughs.

Jake decided gospel music was his life, the world which he was born into, not this faraway world he never understood. The phone calls and the offers only solidified the decision he reached when his world was no larger than a cotton patch.

"God had taken me from that sharecropper farm where I never had anything. He had opened doors for me. To accept those offers would have been saying, 'Lord, thank you for bringing me this far. I'll take it from here on myself.' They were giving me a blank check. But I had a Cadillac and more importantly I had seen people come to the Lord after hearing songs we had sung. I thought of Pop, down on his knees praying for me. I couldn't let him down like that," Jake says.

Looking back, Jake second-guesses nothing. He says he has a little but he needs nothing. "Oh, I need a new heart and I could use a cure for diabetes, but I don't need a thing and don't want a thing. A minister friend of mine told me I could have served the same God in New York that I serve in Georgia. I've always thought that was a myth. When they set a table like that in front of you, there are a lot of temptations and I'm not all that good or holy. God has just used me," he says.

Jerry Crutchfield, one of country music's most renowned producers, says Jake the singer could have made that transition. He is not as sure about Jake the man.

"He could have explored other genre of music. He was so dynamic and expressive. He had the ability. But emotionally, I don't know if Jake could have been truly committed to any

It looks as if Jake is lifting Hovie Lister as they go "Higher and Higher." Such antics were unrehearsed and were criticized by some ministers.

Usually, Elvis would come on stage, tap Jake on the shoulder then sing his part while Jake watched from the wings. This time, Jake sang with Presley and the other Statesmen at the Ellis Auditorium in Memphis, Tennessee.

other kind of music," says Crutchfield, the president of MCA Music Publishing and a longtime friend of Jake's.

None of this altered Elvis Presley's affection for either Jake or the other gospel music people he admired. Over the years, until Colonel Tom Parker stopped him, Elvis used to sneak on stage whenever the Statesmen were at the Ellis Auditorium in Memphis.

"I'd feel a tap on my shoulder and there was Elvis. He always sang my part, but he knew them all," Jake says.

J.D. Sumner confirms what most of the books on Elvis have said. Until Presley's death in 1977, Sumner and the Stamps were behind him on stage so he learned first hand how important gospel music was to the troubled superstar.

"Elvis tried to sing like Jake. That's where he got everything and he would tell you that in a Church of God minute. Jake was his idol. He always wanted Jake to sing with him," Sumner says.

The late Mary Lynch Jarvis, in an interview prior to her death, talked about his influence on Presley. She was the widow of his longtime producer.

"Elvis' goal was to be a gospel singer and to sing like Jake Hess. He got a lot of his hand motions from Jake and the way he shook his leg from Chief," she said.

The Big Chief (James Wetherington) was real close to Elvis. After the Statesmen would sing in Memphis he and a lot of the fellows would head to Graceland.

"Elvis would ask me to go with them, but I never would. Finally one night he asked me why I wouldn't go. I told him, 'Elvis, I don't want your real estate, I don't want a car and I don't even want one of your TCB (Taking Care of Business) pins. I just want your friendship."

"You got it," he told Jake.

He must have meant that, for when Jake was hospitalized after his first open heart surgery, he got a phone call from Las Vegas.

"I understand you're going to be under doctor's care for six weeks. You're going to tell me you won't come out here because of your doctor. But my doctor knows your doctor and he can come with you. I have a suite for you right next to mine. I want you and Joyce to come out here," Elvis said.

Jake said no, an answer that disappointed his doctor, Milton Grossman. "I told Elvis I'd love to see him and that we'd enjoy his show, but that I'd better stay in Nashville," Jake says.

Felton Jarvis called right back. "You don't say no to Elvis," he said.

"I didn't insult him. But the doctors told me not to drive a car or to make any major decisions."

"Elvis made all the decisions for you," Jarvis said.

That was the way Elvis Presley ran his life and that was the way those around him responded. When Jake and the Imperials went into the studio to help back him on his "How Great Thou Art" album, he saw that up close.

Dozens of musicians were on the clock but Elvis and Jake were in the booth talking. This wasn't unusual, for when one of his quartet friends were around he always wanted to talk about the days when he listened to the Statesmen and Blackwood Brothers.

"I really want to sing nothing but gospel," Elvis said.

Mary Lynch Jarvis, center, was married to Felton Jarvis, Elvis Presley's producer. She was also a longtime friend of Jake and Joyce Hess. She died in the summer of 1995.

"Why don't you just do it?" Jake asked. "If anyone in the world has the backing, it's you. You could buy everybody a bus if that's what it took."

Elvis gestured toward the studio where all the musicians were sitting around. "Look at all the people I'd put out of work."

Someone reminded him that those people were getting paid and Elvis reminded him that it was he who was paying all of them. He and Jake went out there and soon they were around the piano. Elvis, always a quick learner, was having trouble with "If I Could See My Mother Pray Again," a song that reminded him of his late mother whom he worshipped.

"I told him to start thinking about her when she was living and he managed to get through it."

During the session, Elvis decided he needed another upbeat song and he asked Jake if his publishing company had one that he could use. The others had been pushing songs all day, but Elvis had fended them away.

Jake suggested "If the Lord Wasn't Walking By My Side." It was a Henry Slaughter tune and he was playing piano on the session.

"Show me how it goes," Elvis said.

The Imperials sang it and after they did, Elvis joined in. They recorded a take and when it was played back you could hear Jake Hess above everyone—including Elvis.

"I gotta back out of there some" Jake said.

Felton Jarvis agreed.

"Leave it just like it is," Elvis said.

"But it'll be a Jake song," Jarvis said.

"That's okay."

For that album, Elvis received his first of two Grammy Awards. Both came for his recordings of gospel music.

Even Priscilla Presley knew about Jake. When she met him, she told how she had to compete with him, how her husband kept a tape player by the bed and every night would play her a favorite Jake Hess recording.

Presley's love of Jake and his music has been documented by most of the books written on him, before and after his death. None emphasized what gospel music meant to him more than "Last Train To Memphis," the definitive biography by Peter Guralnick, published in 1994. He even talked to Dixie Locke, a former girl friend of Presley's who remembered that often their dates were to concerts at Ellis Auditorium.

Elvis, who was a frustrated bass singer, got a lot of his stage mannerisms from the Chief who worked so well with Hovie.

Wrote Guralnick: *"It was the Statesmen who remained their favorites—listen to Jake, Elvis would say to Dixie as he hit yet another thrilling high note with that controlled vibrato and the crowd went wild and called for him to do it again. ... We were so impressed with them, we practically worshipped Jake Hess, we were like groupies, I guess, the quartets were like part of our family."*

In 1995, RCA Victor released a two CD set of gospel music entitled "Amazing Grace," containing a collection of Presley's favorite sacred recordings. With it came a 28-page booklet that was as much a brief history of gospel music as it was a look at Elvis. On the cover of the booklet was a photo of Elvis singing with a quartet which was identified at the Blackwood Brothers. It wasn't. It was the Statesmen and it was a rare photograph that included Jake, who usually left the stage when Presley arrived. The text was written by Charles Wolfe, an English professor at Middle Tennessee University in Murfreesboro, Tennessee.

"These recordings," wrote Wolfe, "serve as an appropriate capstone for the part of his music he returned to over and over again—a part of his music that helped define his style, his career, and the complex personality that changed the face of American culture."

Country singer Larry Gatlin takes that farther. His family has been friends of Jake's since he and his brothers were children. He even had a brief stint with the Imperials after Jake had left the group. He believes the impact of Jake and gospel music has been underestimated.

"If you take it to square one and say Elvis Presley was the single most important figure in the music industry or in American music, who were his influences? Who did he listen to? What kind of music inspired him? So many of us in the music business—be it country, pop, rock 'n' roll or blues, learned to sing sitting in church, singing out of hymnals. So I don't think you can ever truly measure the impact of Jake Hess," Gatlin says.

Never over the years did Jake Hess take advantage of his relationship with Elvis Presley. So when Presley died in 1977, he didn't intend to start. Then J.D. Sumner called and said his bus would pick him up and bring Jake to Memphis, that they would be singing at Presley's funeral.

This wouldn't be the first time Jake had sung at a public funeral. In Memphis, he and the Statesmen sang at services for R.W. Blackwood. Before that, in 1953, the Statesmen had sung at Hank Williams, Sr.'s funeral in Montgomery, Alabama.

"His mother asked us to sing 'Precious Memories' and when we got there Red Foley wanted us to back him up on 'Peace in the Valley.' Roy Acuff was in charge and he asked us to sing 'I Saw the Light.' That was before gospel singers knew that song but he was upset when we said no. He cussed us out but he couldn't do much because Hank's mother had invited us. Country singers were demanding that Roy put them on stage. It was awful," Jake remembers.

J.D. Sumner had been put in charge of Elvis' services. He remembered Presley's favorite songs and he called Jake, Hovie Lister and James Blackwood to join him. That group of legends enjoyed themselves so much that a nugget of an idea was born that afternoon in Memphis.

None of this ever impressed Jake Hess. All he ever wanted was a friend. Whenever he saw Elvis Presley he remembered the awe-struck kid backstage and not the wealthy but unhappy man he became.

Chris and Becky Hess wanted more than that. They were impressed with Elvis. Chris remembered answering the phone at their house in Nashville and hearing the unmistakable voice of Elvis on the other end.

Now they were with their father in Memphis. When they walked up to the auditorium, there were barricades. Elvis was going to be coming past. They found a spot and thought they'd be first in line, that they would get to see Elvis.

Police had made a path for Elvis, but down that path came their father. Chris and Becky told him to join them, that Elvis was coming.

Instead, he motioned for them to follow him and with Jake leading the way, the army of police parted and let them through. Backstage, in a secluded room was Elvis.

Chris Hess remembers what happened. When he tells the story, he even lapses into a voice that mimics Elvis' distinctive baritone.

"We went in this room and there was Elvis and Priscilla. Dad just walks up and says, 'Elvis, I want you to meet my son and my daughter.' He introduced us to Elvis. That was neat. I always thought that was important, but now that I'm older I realize that our Dad introduced us to someone much more important than Elvis and that was Jesus Christ."

When Tammy Wynette married George Richey, the Statesmen sang at their wedding in Jupiter, Florida. Wearing colorful tuxedos, Jake and Hovie Lister head for the ceremony where Jake sang "You Are So Beautiful." Richey once played piano for the Homeland Harmony.

9

"Don't Limit God"

J ake Hess was on a hospital bed. In the distance, was a voice, a woman's voice. He could almost understand what she was saying and he tried to turn up the volume a notch so he could hear her better. She was talking to some other people, faintly telling them they could have saved this patient if they could have gotten his blood pressure up, if they had just been able to stabilize him. Most of what she was saying was technical mumbo-jumbo, but he made out enough of her words to realize that she was talking about him.

Could have saved him, she said.

That got his attention.

He began to remember.

People in white suits ... everywhere ... doctors and nurses ... everybody was talking ... excited yet calm ... equipment filled the room ... tiny lights twinkled ... high-tech beeping sounds throbbed from all those gadgets.

Then he was alone. All the people went away and all of the equipment was carted out of his room. It was quiet. Quiet and dark. The doctors and nurses had given up on him.

Don't do that, he wanted to say, I'm alive, I'm fine. He wanted to yell, but he couldn't. He wanted to move but nothing worked. His mind was giving commands to his hands and arms but no one was home.

How much time had passed he wasn't sure. But there he was, laid out on that bed and again people were crowded all around him, staring down at his lifeless body. It was a group of student nurses, listening to their instructor lecture about this patient they had just lost, how they had found no pulse. When they went away and left him alone, he knew he had to do something to let people know he was alive.

He concentrated on one hand, one finger. He was working as hard to do this one simple thing as he had worked at anything in his life.

His hand moved. Again. A little more.

There was a button next to the bed. He had to push it. He willed that hand to move some more and it did. Closer. More time passed and finally he touched the button.

Hazel Hodges was the nurse who answered the alarm. Locating a faint pulse, she sounded an alarm and the people came out of the walls. Everybody went back to work.

Jake Hess was alive.

He still is. Even though doctors and nurses two other times have said he was dead. When he recites his medical history it is

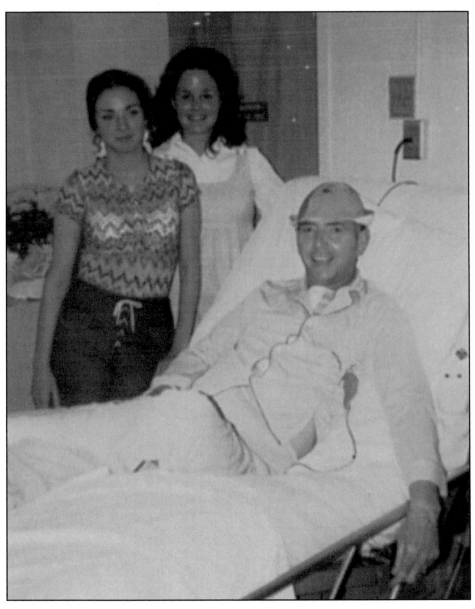

Jake became a familiar patient at Nashville hospitals. Becky and Lani Ruth Morris were visiting so he put on his favorite Disney World hat. He was recovering from his first open heart surgery.

with the emotion of someone reading a phone book out loud. Only the phone book isn't funny and when Jake tells about all his ailments he can make you laugh. The stories are serious, but he isn't.

These things, these "isms" as he calls them, are just part of living, even though they have threatened his life for more than 40 years.

Pericarditis, an inflammation of the sac around the heart. Nephritis, a chronic infection of the kidneys. Numerous heart attacks. Two open-heart surgeries. Cancer of the face. Circulatory problems. Diabetes.

Jake treats his diseases with laughter. For his family and friends, smiles haven't always come that easy.

His daughter Becky remembers his first heart attack. She was 14 and in the hospital waiting room. Her mother said she could go into the room and see him.

"But don't upset him," Joyce said.

"I tried to be pleasant and keep a smile on my face. It did all right until I got ready to leave. Daddy put his arm up over his head and started to cry. I was so afraid. I thought I would never see him again. Even now, he worries me to death every day," she says.

His son Chris remembers the cancer.

"They made him a new lip. I was scared. This was cancer. It's going to eat his whole face off, I figured. I was asking why. I wanted a reason. I said something to Dad about this and he said he didn't know, but that God must have a reason. That was powerful, and that was the man I grew up with," he says.

J.D. Sumner has his own collection of memories. In 1983, when they were on the road together as members of the Masters V, he checked Jake into seven different hospitals. His first memory goes back several years to an early heart attack.

Chris Hess joined his father on the road and finished high school by mail. He not only sang with Jake, he helped check him into hospitals all over the country when his health grew worse.

Joyce Hess had called Mary Sumner and said Jake needed J.D. to get to the hospital. When he got there, Jake could barely talk.

"George, my insurance lapsed yesterday. Get a hold of Nancy Dunne. See what you can do," he whispered.

Dunne has worked for Jake for years. To him, she can do anything. For him, she will try. When Sumner got to her office, she had run out of options.

"I tried to get him to pay that. He had said he was going to do it today. Something has to be done," she said.

Sumner went to work. By securing the funds and working out the details, he was able to preserve Jake's insurance coverage.

"It was like God had done it," says Sumner, who wasn't through. The National Quartet Convention was going on that same week in Memphis. Hopping on his bus, that's where Sumner headed.

Taking the microphone, Sumner talked to the audience that night. It was vintage J.D. He might have been pushing a new record at his table in the rear or he might have been with Jake in some record store, back when they used to banter back and forth to those shop owners. Only there was only little of his usual humor that night.

"I'm not trying to tell you how good I am, because you folks know me too well. But you do know how close Jake and me are and he's in trouble. Do you folks think us gospel singers are rich? We put on a show because you folks want us to put on a show. This suit I'm wearing cost $350. This special made shirt cost $45. This tie $30 and these shoes $100. Course, I got the raggediest underwear of anybody at this convention. Jake Hess ain't here. He's flat on his back in a hospital and his is broke. Flat broke. If you had the chance, would you buy Jake a meal? Of course, you would. So I'm gonna pass a hat and I want you to pretend Jake's here and you're gonna buy him supper," Sumner said.

He collected more than $5,800. There was folding money but there was also lots of coins. People remembered

J.D. Sumner put the money in a burlap sack and on Sunday started back to Nashville. He went straight to the hospital and marched into Jake's room.

He poured out the money on Jake's bed—coins and all.

When J.D. Sumner tells the story like this on himself he injects the humor he shows on the stage. But when he sheds the image and quits playing J.D., tears roll down his cheeks. He explains his 50-year relationship with Jake Hess in very simple terms.

"I love him," he says.

Since 1981, they have worked together on stage on a

Henry Slaughter's liner notes for this album said for Jake's children—Becky and Chris—to "grow up loving their father and his work" is the highest compliment anyone can pay.

As boys growing up in Texas, Rudy, Larry and Steve were big fans of the Statesmen and the Blackwoods. All grown up, the Gatlin Brothers joined the Masters V for an old gospel number.

regular basis. For seven years, they were part of the Masters V, a quartet that assembled a lot of gospel music history.

J.D. Sumner on bass. Rosie Rozell on tenor. Hovie Lister on piano. James Blackwood and Jake sharing the lead and baritone parts. Part Statesmen, part Blackwoods and 100 percent fun. It was old friends singing old songs for audiences that included faces old and new.

Jake was on the West Coast singing with Dr. Gene Scott when Lister and Sumner called. He arranged for them to come out to Los Angeles and booked them on Scott's television show, where he was the music director. For several days, the five of them sang on the show, rehearsing as they sang. It was an opportunity for them to get paid to practice.

This wasn't going to be as easy as it sounded. Every one of them in the group had led his own group, so they had to designate someone to be in charge. It was understood that Lister would be the manager with Blackwood as his assistant.

Material wasn't an issue. Each of them had signature songs that people wanted to hear and those songs were almost enough to fill a booking themselves.

"When James sang lead, we sounded like the Blackwoods. When I sang lead, we sounded like the Statesmen," Jake says.

The major problem was age and health. At the outset, they decided they would only sing on weekends or else just a few nights a week. Nothing too taxing, for there were enough

Dr. Charles Stanley, center, pastor of the First Baptist Church in Atlanta, welcomed The Masters V—Rosie Rozell, Hovie Lister, James Blackwood, J.D. Sumner and Jake Hess.

bypasses in the group to build an expressway. But once they were on the road and once they heard the applause, all of that changed.

It seemed so easy.

"It was something we could do without starting at the bottom. Everybody wants a chance to do it all over again and that was our chance," Jake remembers.

It was anything but easy. Being on the road and living on a bus doesn't come naturally for a young man. It tests you physically and emotionally. And these men were well into their fifties.

"We drove ourselves into the ground. What we should have done was stay out two or three nights a week and said no to everything else. But we were like a bunch of teenagers. We forgot everything we had set out to do. You don't have any

Yes, there are six Masters V members singing on this number. The extra member was Chris Hess who at times stood in for his father and often for an ailing James Blackwood.

sense when you are doing something you love as much as all of us loved singing," Jake says.

Rozell had a stroke in 1983. He was replaced by Steve Warren, who had once bragged to Hovie Lister that if he was ever needed he could sing every part except bass. They were in Texas when Rozell was taken to the hospital. Warren lived nearby so he got the call. "Wear a blue suit and be there at 6:30 p.m.," Lister told him. That night, he sang tenor and never missed a cue or a lyric.

He had a job, but it probably was more than he dreamed of it being. He sang and arranged but he also unloaded all of the heavy equipment from the bus and it was he who had to do anything the aging Quartet Men around him could not.

Still, as Warren discovered, they enjoyed each other.

They had been on the road 48 days and the final date was at the Joyful Noise, a Christian club in East Point, Georgia.

"I'd call a song and Jake and J.D. would be laughing. I kept trying to bring it back and they would laugh some more. It was those two, but I thought, 'Surely, James is not doing it.' But lo and behold, he was laughing, too. I called 'Prayer Is the Key.' Surely they'll get serious on that one, but they blew that, too. Finally they all left the stage. Only Steve Warren was left out there," Hovie Lister says.

They were laughing but they were also hurting. His son Chris had to stand in for Blackwood on baritone for awhile, and for a time Jake Hess Jr. traveled with the Masters V as their road manager. He remembers being on stage with his father holding up Rosie and James holding up Jake.

"When I got home, I was sick. You travel with that many sick men and you get down. People who came to the shows didn't know any of this. They didn't know what all of them went through just to sing," Jake Jr. says.

Years before, Roy Acuff had chided the Statesmen Quartet at Hank Williams Sr.'s funeral for not knowing "I Saw the Light." That was forgotten when he joined Hovie Lister, Jake and the Masters V on the Grand Ole Opry.

It was their collective health that finally led to the Masters V being disbanded in 1988. By then, the group was down to only Lister and Sumner. But in the beginning, they were a dream team, winning a Grammy Award in 1981 for their very first album. One by one, however, the Masters V learned they were not masters of their own health.

In 1983, Sumner checked Jake into seven different hospitals in seven different cities. One of them was in Macon, Georgia, where a doctor said there was no muscle left in his heart. Another was in Fort Valley, Georgia, a town that is known more for growing peaches than its medical facilities.

That was nothing new for Jake. He had a similar experience when he was traveling with his children a few years before the Masters V.

The Sound of Youth was in Houston, a town noted for its work in heart disease. They were on their way to Fort Worth and had stopped at Denny's Restaurant for a quick meal. Chris Hess looked at his father and ran off the bus looking for his sister.

"He was as white as a sheet and he could hardly talk where you could understand him. I got come of the other fellows and we wanted to get him to a hospital there in Houston. Dad gave us his 'nothin' but fine' routine and convinced us we should go on," he said.

Steve Warren, left, bragged he knew all the parts except bass. When he took over as tenor, he had to do more than sing, for he soon learned he was the healthiest member of the group.

Jake had just finished a number on Bill Gaither's "Old Friends" video when Vestal Goodman interrupted the music. She wanted to pray for Jake, who was obviously frail and weak. She asked the Lord to help her neighbor from North Alabama recover to sing some more since the world still needed him and his music.

Somewhere on the road to Fort Worth, Billy Grammer woke up. He had been asleep when they stopped. Grammer, a Grand Ole Opry star, was traveling with the group at the time. He looked at Jake and said they had better stop, that Jake was in serious trouble.

They were in Huntsville, Texas. A large prison was located there which meant the local hospital was well equipped. They might have had the equipment, but they were short on doctors who knew anything about the heart.

"Nurses got his pills and I saw them with medical books trying to match the pills to the pictures in the books. I lost it. I wanted them to do something," daughter Becky Buck says.

Jake was hooked up to monitors and the results were radioed to Chicago where a specialist was on the phone, giving instructions.

A diagnosis finally came from Chicago.

The man was either having a heart attack or had had one.

"I thought I was dying for sure, but there was nothing I could do," Jake says.

Long ago, Jake Hess turned his health over to Someone more powerful than a medical doctor. Friends would check him into a hospital and doctors would do their job. But his doctor was the Lord.

He decided that many years ago when he was in an Atlanta hospital with nephritis, the disease that seemed to start it all. The Statesmen had been at a small town in Louisiana when Jake got so swollen that he couldn't put on his shoes or button his pants. A squad car rushed him to Houston where he caught a plane for Atlanta. He had to be carried from the plane like a sack of flour.

Doctors didn't know what was wrong and they told Joyce Hess that it didn't look good. A local church group was visiting the hospital and when they saw Joyce and how upset she was they turned Jake's room into a prayer meeting. They got to shouting and one woman broke a chair. He needed to be quiet so nurses soon ushered that group out of the room so he could rest. Joyce left with them and went home to check on the kids.

A young man he had never seen came to the door.

"Can I come in?" he asked.

"Sure. Welcome to Grand Central Station," Jake said.

The boy stood by his bed.

"I heard you had been having excitement here. You don't know me, but I know you. I'd like to pray for you. Everybody else has been praying for you to go. I'd like to pray for you to stay. I think the Lord has something left for you to do," he said.

The prayer was short and simple.

Then he left.

Jake had something to tell Joyce so he picked up the phone. He told her he was fine. She started to cry, remembering how pessimistic the doctors had been. Jake insisted he was fine. He even told her to mark the calendar, that he would be home on a particular day.

Jake never saw that young fellow again. He learned that he was a student at Columbia Theology School in Atlanta and that he worked part-time at a radio station. That's all Jake knew.

"God healed me," Jake says. "I was drowning in my own fluids but God healed me."

Not long after that, he was released from the hospital and the children threw a party celebrating his being home. He looked at the calendar.

"Look at this Joyce. It's the date I told you I'd be home."

Many years after that prayer in the hospital, Vestal Goodman offered another prayer on his behalf. It was during a taping for "Old Friends," an early video in Bill Gaither's Homecoming series of gospel music tapes. The studio was filled with gospel music stars, people who had known one another before they owned a bus or before they bought a new head of hair.

Jake had just sung a song. Cameras tell the truth. Anyone who watches that video knows that Jake Hess was not a well man. He looked thin and frail. The song didn't give it away. His face did.

He was not only down physically. His emotions also were in pain. Doctors had told him to quit the road or he would die.

He was facing a decision he didn't relish. Jake couldn't imagine living without singing.

Doctors told him in 1993 that there was nothing left to do. They talked about his heart and about his life on the road. They told him he shouldn't be putting his body through all of that.

"As of when?" Jake asked.

"As of today," the doctor said.

"What about Birmingham? We're booked in Birmingham."

"Jake, it's the Birminghams in your life that are going to kill you."

All of this news seemed to be written on his face that day in the crowded studio as he finished singing about how he loved Jesus. Vestal Goodman, who has been his friend since her late brother, Cat Freeman, brought him to their family's farm, came toward him.

She stopped the music and asked everyone in the room to reach out their hands to Jake. Then she asked God to spare her friend and keep him singing.

"Leave him with us and let him continue to bless," she prayed.

She remembers that moment vividly.

"I loved Jake so much and I sensed how desperately the world needed to hear Jake Hess. I prayed for God to hold him, to heal him and to keep him singing. He's not old enough to leave, not this early. That day, I felt we were in a room full of people who loved Jake. I felt in my heart that this was the time to pray, to bind that room together for there is strength in numbers. If enough of us said, 'Let us keep him. Let us keep him for You know how much the world needs this man.' Surely the Lord would listen," Goodman says.

Jake Hess never thought Gaither would include that

moment on the video, but he did, and people who watch it still talk about the power of her prayer and the sincere love between people captured on tape.

"I thought Bill would delete it. Vestal is a dear friend. We've known each other since we were kids. When she started to pray, I thought, 'That's not on the program.' I knew I would cry and when I do, I am the ugliest man in the world. When the Lord starts blessing me I'm either going to cry or laugh and I don't know which. But I am definitely not ashamed of that being on television. I'm a Christian, and I want the world to know it," he says.

Right after Vestal Goodman prayed for him, Jake was back at the microphone to do a song he had performed thousands of times. It was Mosie Lister's "Then I Met the Master." Jake, not the Statesmen, recorded it with Wally Varner on the keyboard. He started with the second verse and was having trouble with the lyrics.

From the bleachers came James Blackwood. They stood there, two old friends as the title of the video would indicate. Soon Glen Payne of the Cathedrals made it a trio, a trio that combined had more than 150 years in gospel music.

Blackwood saw the emotions building that day.

"Anyone who has gone through the troubles he has, and faced death, with as big a heart as Jake has, you become more emotional. It's natural, from the Lord dealing with you, from your family, from the people you love. I appreciate anyone who can show their emotions. Some people brag they've never cried but that isn't a compliment to me. It takes a big person to cry. Jake does and so does J.D. People think he's such a big bear of a person, but he's a softie," Blackwood said.

Jake didn't always want to show those feelings. But with one ailment and "ism" after another coming his way, people

Vestal Goodman, right, has known Jake since her brother, Cat Freeman, brought him home to their farm. Lily Fern Weatherford remembers how kind Jake was to her when she joined her late husband's group as one of the few females in a gospel quartet.

began to routinely ask him how he was feeling. People who didn't know him. People who didn't need to know all of the details. Jake isn't sure where he came up with the phrase, but for the past 35 years, when someone has asked how he was feeling, he would say "Nothin' but fine."

"We've heard that all our lives," Chris Hess says.

"Nothin' but fine in cardiac care units. Nothin but fine when it's cancer. Nothin but fine with diabetes. I remember singing on TV with Dad and we were singing a song he had sung for years and he was missing the words. We finished and off the air I asked what he was doing. He said it was kind of hard to sing with a nitroglycerine tablet in your mouth. So it is also nothin' but fine when he's on stage."

Jake Hess can't forget what Armond Morales told him in the months leading up to the creation of the Imperials in 1963. "Don't limit God," he said. So every time there is bad news, he has faith that God will take care of it.

Vestal Goodman saw him in 1994 after doctors at Emory University in Atlanta had told him he was not a candidate for a heart transplant, that they considered no one over the age of 65.

Goodman knew that when she sat down next to him.

"I asked him how he was feeling. He started to cry. He put his arm around me and he told me that he had gotten some bad news. 'But how do you feel?' I asked. He smiled that smile and said that he actually felt better than he had in a long time. I know Joyce, Becky, Chris, Jake Jr. and those beautiful grandchildren need Jake. And God surely does love Jake because he's such a darling. They all need him, but the world also needs him."

*While the cameras are rolling, Jake shares a laugh
with George Younce as Bob Cain sings his song.*

10

A Studio Filled With Love

Lon Varnell had planned his own funeral. He didn't want his wife to be embarrassed by the size of the crowd so the outrageous basketball official and coach had put it together himself. Jake Hess had been booked to sing. The service might have been unorthodox but for him to be singing over wood wasn't unusual. He did it often. Varnell handled everything well but the timing—for that same afternoon a lot of Jake's buddies were in town to sing a song with Bill Gaither.

Gaither composes beautiful choral anthems and over the years earned a well-deserved reputation for the music he writes.

It is sacred but it is classical in the way it is arranged. The former Indiana schoolteacher never seems to be off from work. His busy mind refuses to take a holiday.

Twenty-five years ago, the Bill Gaither Trio often sang on the gospel circuit. It was Bill, his wife Gloria and his brother Danny. His love for quartet music went back to his childhood when his father used to take him to the Ryman Auditorium in Nashville. Now he was back in Nashville, with a room full of technology that groups he saw the first time he came would never understand. In the past, they hauled their Silvertone sound system from Sears around in the trunk of a car. Now every group sets up a stage that looks like the showroom of a music store.

That all went into his decision to invite a lineup of Southern gospel singers to the Master's Touch Studio in February of 1991. Gaither worked too hard and he needed a hobby. Maybe his childhood interest in gospel music could be turned into one. Out of his trio grew the Gaither Vocal Band, a group aptly named since their voices turn into instruments when they sing. Gaither wanted them to see and hear some of the singers he was always telling them about.

Nothing elaborate was planned. The Vocal Band had put down a track for an old Stamp-Baxter number, "Where Could I Go But to the Lord?" and his guest list was going to join them. The video camera was an after-thought, there for history rather than sales.

Jake got there after 4 o'clock that afternoon.

"When I opened the door, it hit me. It was the shock of a lifetime. Everybody was so free. Everybody was telling each other they loved them. It was a spiritual happening. I didn't see any cameras even. All I saw was love," Jake says.

Recording "Where Could I Go?" took very little time. It is only eight measures of music, a song some of those people

sang when it was new.
Gaither had sandwiches
brought in and after they ate a
photographer was going to set
up a group picture of them.

Larry and Rudy Gatlin
were there with the old-
timers. They are two-thirds of
country music's Gatlin Brothers. They grew up around
these folks. Jake remembers
the first time he heard the
brothers singing back in
Texas, they were so small that
Rudy Gatlin fell off of the Dr.
Pepper crate he was standing
on to reach the microphone.
That afternoon in Nashville,
Larry Gatlin told someone that

*When Bill Gaither is in the
studio, there is no doubt
who is in charge.*

if a bomb dropped on that studio all of his heroes would be killed.

A lot of heroes were there: Glen Payne and George
Younce of the Cathedrals, Howard and Vestal Goodman, James
Blackwood, Hovie Lister, Eva Mae LeFevre, Jim Hill, Buck
Rambo, Jim Murray, Brock and Ben Speer along with the Speer
sisters, Mary Tom Reid and Rosa Nell Powell.

Gatlin describes what happened as lunch was finished.

"I was sitting on the piano bench when Eva Mae LeFevre
sat down next to me. I wasn't going to pass up an opportunity
like that so I asked her to play something for me. She started
playing and about that time James (Blackwood) walked up and
Jake came in. I told the guy in the studio to get the camera
rolling," Gatlin says.

Jake always has fun when he's around two of his favorite bass singers and favorite people—J.D. Sumner, above, and George Younce.

Jim Hill was still eating when he heard the singing begin. He joined the others who were congregating in the studio.

"People in the studio began to see something was happening, that they needed to get this down on tape. They must have figured that they would never have that chance again, with so many legends together in one room. The Lord began to bless and tears began to flow," Hill says.

There was only one camera. Unlike the video series that was spawned that day, this was primitive television. One camera and questionable sound. Yet, Gaither's crew must have known they were seeing something special for instead of being an audience, they went to work.

George Younce says everything was off the cuff.

"We went in to do one song. But do you know what was going on in that room? More than any of the other videos even, it was absolute love for each other. We were hugging necks. We went in to do one song, but I looked around and saw guys I had rubbed elbows with all these years, guys I loved, and there was love going on. The main thing, for those six hours, was love. We decided to ad lib a few songs and we had been singing for a long time before I realized the cameras were rolling. I forgot the words to a song I heard Big Chief do every night for years and you know who fed me the words? Larry Gatlin. He's in country music, but he knew every word," Younce says.

There was love, and some of the people who were loving were not always so lovable. Gaither has said that just because these people sing about the love of God doesn't mean they always try to emulate it. They have memories as long as their buses and some of them remember a night in Waycross when that other fellow took more than his time on stage. For an outsider that may be trivial, but to a Quartet Man these are the things from which feuds are born.

Gospel music people take on the characteristics of a family. They bicker. They gossip. They hold grudges. This was their family reunion, and a lot of ancient wounds began to heal while they stood around that piano.

"The Lord produced that video—through Bill Gaither," Jake says.

"It's the songs. These are great songs. Bill says great songs are great songs forever. They don't wear out. The videos have those great songs plus the love and the spirit you feel. I have never seen a coming together such as you see when we get in that studio," says Ben Speer, who has been music director of the series that began that day in Nashville.

"Nobody else could weave that magic like Bill Gaither," Younce says.

Jake and Hovie.

Even when the camera is on, you never know where Bill Gaither will land. Sometimes he goes into the crowd to help sing a favorite song joining Faye and Brock Speer and Jake.

Jake didn't know any of that when he joined the others. He didn't notice the cameras. "If I had, I wouldn't have been butting in on everybody else's songs," he says. Even when he did notice them recording, he thought it would be something for Bill and Gloria to watch by the fireplace at night.

In that log cabin studio, there was genuine affection and there were moments to savor. Gatlin mimicking Jake. Younce doing an impersonation of Big Chief. Vestal Goodman praying for songwriter Dottie Rambo, who was too ill to be there.

"You don't usually have a service like that in a recording studio. That was a special day with special people," Jake says.

Jake didn't get to perform or visit with these friends the way he once did. Every Saturday, he was flying out to California to sing at Sunday Services with Dr. Gene Scott. He had done some vocal work for the Baptist Sunday School Board. He

After watching footage of the first video, Bill Gaither suggested a revitalized Statesmen Quartet. Naturally Jake and Hovie were there and they were joined by Johnny Cook, Biney English and Bob Caldwell. They became the 1992 model Statesmen.

had had a syndicated television show. That afternoon, he did some of the songs everyone remembered. Mainly he had fun.

Gaither also had fun. His enjoyment exploded when he not only listened to the music but watched the video footage. He had invited his heroes and the Lord had come along for the singing.

Two things came out of that afternoon.

Gaither decided to produce a one-hour video on their jam session and from that crude beginning would soon come his Homecoming video series. After the video album was previewed on Pat Robertson's 700 Club, people scrambled to get a copy.

That day also marked the rebirth of the Statesmen. The group had essentially disbanded 12 years before when Lister went into the Masters V in 1980. Remembering the excitement he felt when he heard the original group sing in 1950, Gaither thought people would welcome their return.

"I thought it would work. When I heard Jake sing that day, I marveled at the power. The next day, I called Hovie and told him he ought to consider uniting the Statesmen," Gaither says.

Then he called Jake.

"He said it would be nice for us to get back together again. He said Hovie and I ought to talk. He also had a backer for us," Jake says.

Gaither helped them find the younger voices that would be required to make this project work. They settled on Johnny Cook as the tenor, Biney English as the baritone and Bob Caldwell as the bass singer. They went into the studio to cut an album. In early 1992, they sang their first job as the Statesmen.

Jake says the sound wasn't there.

"It's hard to get a Statesmen sound. We just weren't what people expected us to be. We went to music tracks. It helped in

Old singers tell old stories. Jake could hear them from George Younce and Hovie Lister. On that couch below, J.D. Sumner shows Rex Nelon, James Blackwood and Lister how a firecracker almost blew away his nose.

Neither Jake nor J.D. Sumner could believe it when after all these years, they saw Hovie Lister get ready to climb up on his piano bench. On the right, Jake is singing but notice he's not looking at David Reece. If he did, his old TV buddy might have made him laugh.

some ways, but Hovie played very little, which old fans resented. It was a different world for him. I can't explain why, but we didn't have a Statesmen sound," he says.

The five of them didn't even live in the same town. They only got together when there was a job. They had O'Neill Terry driving the bus. They sang the same songs and had the same name. That was it.

Hardly a year later, Jake Hess was once again told by a doctor that he had to leave the road. In June of 1993, he did just that. He didn't need a medical degree to know he needed rest. His body told him that every morning.

Heart troubles had plagued him for a long time. Now diabetes was sapping his endurance. He and Joyce decided he needed to get away from the spotlight and the temptation to sing just one more job.

Their daughter Becky had married Brent Buck, a successful businessman in Columbus, Georgia. When she moved and took with her their grand-daughter, Emmy Shea, they began to consider a move back to Georgia themselves. When little Brent was born, that sealed the deal. Jake and Joyce knew if they didn't move, they'd be constantly packing and unpacking from trips to see Becky and the grand-children.

Jake always had been an avid golfer so they found a lot on a golf development in Columbus. "I always prayed I'd one day live on a golf course. I just forgot to pray for the health to play," Jake says.

While their house was being built, they lived on a secluded lake 15 miles out of Columbus. For many people, it would be an idyllic setting. For Jake Hess, it became a prison.

The phone wasn't listed in his name so no one could call, which was horrible to a man who thinks the ringing of a phone is beautiful music. When the phone didn't ring, he began to

*Chris Hess, right, thanked his gospel music
friends for always being there for his Dad
and their family over the years.*

think no one wanted to talk to him anymore. Out in the pine
trees, there were few visitors and Jake began to lock himself
away in the house.

Before he moved to rural Georgia, he had participated in
more rounds of video sessions with Gaither and his other gospel
friends. Gaither had touched a nerve with people who remembered 78 rpm records. He was also finding that the video generation was putting them into their VCRs. Not for nostalgia.
They had never seen a Jake or a Vestal before. All of the old
was new to them.

Gaither was experiencing this every day but he knew he
had to find a way for Jake to know. He was concerned about his
friend. Not because of his "isms," but because of they way his
voice sounded on the phone.

Everyone came to their feet for this one. That's Bill Gaither at the piano and the singers at the mikes include Hovie Lister, Vestal Goodman, Johnny Cook and Jake.

"I thought nobody cared," Jake says.

Bob Terrell, a columnist for The Singing News, did and unusual thing. He put Jake's phone number and address in a column in the magazine. Gaither did the same thing in his monthly newsletter.

"Normally, I would never do something like that. But I wanted him to get some of the calls and letters that we had been getting," Gaither says.

It was a revelation for Jake.

"Had it not been for the Gaither videos, I never would have known that there were people out there who still loved Jake Hess," he says.

Jake has played a vital role in an unexpected phenomenon. Those videos are electronic evangelists. They are carrying an art that was fading into homes that never knew it existed. They are entertaining people who may accidentally learn there is a message in the rhythm. They are sermons that can be played over and over again.

Gaither started with his own heroes. Now he has to share them. Vestal Goodman says she now sings to an entirely new audience.

"Those videos are bringing this type of gospel music full circle. It will come back to the front. Because they see Jake sing, many a young man will say, 'I could sing like that. I want to try.' And God grant that some of the girls may look at some of us and say the same thing. I pray to God they will try, because this is a music that must be kept alive. Bill Gaither is doing that," she says.

Younce has been singing nearly 50 years and now, because of the videos, he is realizing that he was never able to scratch the surface. He had traveled many miles, but a lot of people didn't know he had even left home. Now they do.

"Nobody in the world, nobody in gospel music, could have said to us old-timers, come and do this with me, except Bill Gaither. I get emotional when I talk about him because nobody has reached out to me and Glen like Bill Gaither. He's not doing it for himself. He said he had watched a video where they were documenting the history of country music. He thought about gospel music, and he realized all of that history was going to be gone without anyone putting it down. He didn't say that when he first called. He just said come," Younce says.

Gaither's videos continue to sell. Each one outselling the previous one. In addition to the Homecoming series, he has begun a Hall of Honor series which includes a biographical video on Jake Hess.. To Jake's family, these are not the important facts about the videos.

After moving to Georgia, Jake thought everyone had forgotten him. He didn't know that people still loved him. Through Bill Gaither's popular series of gospel videos, a new generation has discovered him and his singing. That series includes a biographical tape on Jake's life and career. Its taping was a emotional experience for both Jake and Joyce.

"God has opened another door," Chris Hess says.

"The fruits of all he's done are coming back to him," Becky Buck believes.

Jake is more basic.

"They've saved my life."

After he found out Jake Hess was still alive, Terry Bradshaw, left, wanted to meet the singer who was his boyhood favorite. Their conversation on the telephone turned into a friendship then a recording session where Jake found out the NFL Hall of Famer knew the lyrics to old gospel songs as well as he did.

11

Coming Home to Sing

The frail man who moved to this town to end his career and his life was almost forgotten. Walking the Columbus stage that evening, invigorated by a robust robed choir that stood behind him, Jake Hess was home. Three generations of his family were there. So was his doctor, his druggist, his mechanic and his tailor. So was the man who sells him his hair. The mayor of Columbus came, along with a crowd that set a record for the brand new Columbus Civic Center. So was Bill Gaither and The Vocal Band, guys that Jake laughingly refers to as his backup group. So was Judy Martin, who soon would become his daughter-in-law. So was Hovie and Vestal and Howard, old friends who knew him when his range was greater and his voice was stronger. Only this Friday night in Georgia wasn't about age or health or memories, this night was about love.

"I love you," Jake told the crowd. "I've been telling Brother Bill what a great city Columbus is. Thanks for not making me a liar."

Mayor Bobby Peters proclaimed September 6, 1996 as Jake Hess Day in Columbus and he read a proclamation that night with Jake standing nervously at his side. More than 200 people from Jake's church, Wynnbrook Baptist, came to help him celebrate, but Gaither reminded the Georgia audience that Jake was only on loan to them.

"I know he's a citizen of Columbus," Gaither said. "He's your neighbor, but he is a citizen of the world."

Still, it was fitting that a year of miracles should include that night in that city and that state. Georgia has always been important to Jake Hess. He came

A ticket stub reading:

```
F L O O R
SEC   ROW   SEAT
      1    15

ADMIT ONE THIS DATE ONLY

PREMIER
PRODUCTIONS
PRESENTS
BILL GAITHER
& FRIENDS
WITH
JAKE HESS
COLUMBUS
CIVIC CENTER
COLUMBUS, GA
FRIDAY
SEPT  6, 1996
7:30 PM

NO REFUND PRICE NO EXCHANGE

$18.50
F L O O R
SEC   ROW   SEAT
      1    15

BILL GAITHER
$18.50

      1    15

SEPT  6, 1996
```

Bill Gaither put the show together, but it was Jake Hess Day when they came to Columbus, Georgia in the fall of 1996. The mayor of the city was there and the governor of the state sent a proclamation that was delivered by Hovie Lister. Packing the Columbus Civic Center were more than 10,000 other friends of gospel music, setting an attendance record for the new facility.

Earlier in the evening, they were on the stage with other groups. But how could James Blackwood, Hovie Lister, Jake and J.D. Sumner be together without recreating the excitement of The Masters V. They represent more than two centuries of friendship, fun and gospel music.

there to join the Statesmen and their first singing engagement was in this state. He and Joyce's first home was in Atlanta and their three children were born there. At their Atlanta home, The Imperials got together in the same room for the first time.

Columbus had revitalized him. More than a year earlier, sitting on a bus in Atlanta, Jake and a friend talked with Gaither about doing a concert in the new facility in Columbus. Even then, Jake was doing only one song at a time, often sitting on a stool. He was working selected dates with Gaither, but more often than not, he was singing small churches in Georgia with Chris, his eldest son. No one in that bus parked at the rear of the Atlanta Civic Center imagined that in September of 1996, Jake would be ending the most successful of his 50 years singing gospel music.

"What he does is really powerful. It's an answer to prayer," Gaither says. "Five or six years ago, when we were doing a new Statesmen album, Jake was so shaky that I didn't think he'd make it. If you had told me then that he would put on 30 pounds and sing the way he's singing now, I wouldn't have believed you. Now, I put my arm around him and that is a man. This is a remarkable, living miracle."

Five or six years ago, Jake Hess also had doubts. He was a Quartet Man, not a soloist. Even if he was healthy, he didn't know if audiences would accept him without three voices around him. When he moved into that lakefront house in secluded Juniper, Georgia, he was retired and he was resigned. He was praying for God's will and so were his family and his friends. People around the world wanted him to sing and so did the Lord. Now Jake enjoys today, not worrying about yesterday.

That's part of Jake's spirit, Gaither says. "Jake doesn't look behind him. Others look at him as a kind of monument. Jake looks ahead, to what he's doing tomorrow."

What he's doing today is what he has always done—sing. Not only does he have a regular chair on the stage when Gaither records his ever-popular videos, but he has been busy in the studio, recording two albums in 1996 with another planned for early 1997. He has become a fixture on the Gaither tour, a schedule that in 1997 will take him to Europe for the first time. In 1996, the Gaither video—*Jus' Jake*—was nominated as video of the year by The Singing News. Jake is also planning a one-man show called simply, *"An Evening with Jake."* He is mulling over an idea for a television show. He is excited about a CD that restores the music and the sound of the original Statesmen. He is the busiest retired gospel singer in the business.

"I moved to Georgia to die," Jake says, matter-of-factly. "The medical profession told me I couldn't sing anymore, but

God has allowed me to come back. I'm working as hard now as I have in my life and enjoying it more. We're right in the middle of the good ole days. The Lord has opened so many doors for me—doors I didn't even know were there."

One of those doors was almost in his backyard. The North Highland Assembly of God church is a short walk from Jake's home. When he was singing with the Masters V, they sang in that sanctuary, at a time when Steve Warren not only sang tenor but unloaded most of the equipment since the others were too ill. Soon after he moved to Columbus, Jake heard of a choral concert at the church and he slipped in to listen.

"I thought to myself how much I'd like to sing with that choir," Jake says, not knowing that director Greg Kennard's parents years ago were members of Jim Wetherington's choirs at an Atlanta church.

"My dad must own every album the Statesmen ever made," Kennard says. "I grew up playing the drums behind their records."

Early in 1996, remembering how impressed he was with the North Highland choir, he called Kennard and talked about them working on an album with him. From that conversation came *Leanin'*, a collection of old hymns that sounds very little like they do at 11 o'clock on Sunday morning.

Because of the jazzy, big band sounds, some have said it is Frank Sinatra doing church music. Kennard says it was just an effort to do something new—something Jake Hess has always been fond of doing, even though he says the project was not an old man trying to be cool.

The arrangements and the production were Kennard's. He was looking for a unique sound. "I don't like to do something that's already been done. If people want a dime-a-dozen hymns album they should buy something else. We knew we were going to shock some of his traditional fans, but Jake said 'Don't worry. I like it.' Being a pioneer to him is nothing new. He's always been on the cutting, bleeding edge."

So it was when Terry Bradshaw called. A friend of Jake's, Mickey Vaughn, had read an article about the former Pittsburgh Steeler quarterback in the Dallas newspaper. The reporter asked what Bradshaw's favorite music was and he said gospel. His favorite group was the Statesmen. Vaughn called and brought him up to date on the quartet and their one-time lead singer.

Bradshaw thought Jake Hess was dead.

Soon afterward, the two legends started a telephone friendship. Jake didn't know it at the time, but Bradshaw had recorded a couple of country music albums years ago. Now he wanted to do a gospel album—with Jake.

"Are you going to do something about this or am I?" Bradshaw asked.

Jake finally took him seriously and they began talking about people they knew in the recording industry. Both had been produced by Jerry Crutchfield, the president of MCA Music Publishing, who became interested in the unlikely duo.

"I had never even heard Terry sing, but I knew I liked him. He's tough as nails but a beautiful person. He had been one of my favorite athletes and I enjoyed him as a a football announcer on the Fox Network," Jake says.

With Crutchfield's guiding hand and ear, they went into the studio and recorded *"Jake and Terry."* For Bradshaw, it wasn't work. It was a chance to sing the music he loved with a singer he grew up with. The Hall of Fame quarterback even made an appearance on a Gaither video. On the tape, he seemed as relaxed as his singing partner. That night, it was a different story.

This was a man who made a career of dodging runaway linebackers, but waiting to sing in Fort Worth, Texas, Bradshaw was nervous. Guy Penrod, the lanky lead singer of The Gaither Vocal Band sensed his uneasiness, even though the two men had never met.

"He just walked over to me, put his arms around me and said, 'Let's pray.' And I felt something," Bradshaw says. When he finally went on to the stage of the Tarrant County Convention Center to sing his duet with Jake, he was loose. Jake says Bradshaw is a man who knows how to relax.

Years ago, Greg Kennard's parents sang in a choir directed by the Big Chief, Jim Wetherington. Now Kennard is choir director at North Highland Assembly of God Church in Columbus, Georgia. Kennard produced and arranged "Leanin'", a unique album of old choir book favorites. His rousing choir backed up Jake, both on the album and at the concert where Jake was honored in his adopted hometown.

"Let me tell you, in the studio some of us got to talking about the arrangements. Terry took off his shoes and laid flat on the hardwood floor. He was asleep in less than two minutes. I mean he was snoring. He wasn't faking. He was resting. I've never seen anybody so relaxed," Jake laughs.

Bradshaw wasn't the first singer influenced by Jake. Years ago, Ed Enoch had that same experience. Enoch was part of the Music City Singers and the group was on its way back to Nashville. Enoch, now the lead singer of the Stamps Quartet, was driving the bus. It was 4 in the morning and they were pushing it to get back in time for Jake's 6 a.m. television show.

The conversation turned to Enoch's performance earlier that night on "How Great Thou Art," a piece of music he still considers a signature song. Jake was saying what a great voice he had.

"But you have to see the picture," Jake said.

As they drove, Jake explained. It is a story Enoch has never forgotten. "You sing great, he told me, but you don't see the picture. You have to see that old piece of matted wood. See a drop of blood and see it trickle down. See that one drop that cleanses you from your sin. See those splinters in that cross. If you can see the splinters, then you can relate to the cross."

From the time he went on the road with the John Daniel Quartet until now, Jake Hess has tried to see that cross. This is part of that spirit Gaither talks about. This is one of the reasons people he has never met come up to him in restaurants, call him on the phone or knock on his door. He's reachable. He communicates. He isn't a minister, but through his music he ministers. Such descriptions make him uncomfortable. He sings. He doesn't preach—which is the way he wants it to be.

He wanted it that way years ago when he was flying home from his brother Butch's funeral in Florida. He had been on the road, had been up three nights in a row and was just plain tired. He upgraded to first class so he would have more room to sleep.

Talking was not on Jake's agenda.

The Ivy Leaguer in the next seat had other ideas.

"I'm in computers. What do you do?"

"I'm a musician," Jake said.

That might have ended it had a flight attendant not recognized Jake from TV. She excitedly said that she had prayed she would one day get to meet Jake Hess.

"Then you're a preacher," the fellow said.

"No, just a gospel singer.

A meal was served and in those days a pack of Winstons was on the tray. Jake offered the cigarettes to his seat mate along with the complimentary glass of champagne first class passengers were given.

"See, you are a preacher," the fellow said. "And if you are, then why don't you try and save me."

"I'm not in the saving business. Jesus is in the saving business. I'm just a gospel singer."

The fellow bragged that Billy Graham and Oral Roberts had both tried to save him but neither had been successful. All the time he was laughing at Jake. More taunts followed, but finally Jake managed to fall asleep. Only the man wasn't through.

"You could save me if you wanted to."

"I don't want to," a weary Jake said. "I'm tired, I'm sleepy and I don't want to fool with you."

The man asked why Jake wouldn't pray for him and he told him that he should pray for himself. He confessed that he didn't know how.

"Just talk. Just talk to the Lord," Jake said, explaining the plan of salvation.

In a few minutes, they prayed together and the annoying fellow in the next seat accepted Christ. Several weeks later, Nancy Dunne relayed a letter to Jake that had come from Colorado. The man from the plane said he was going to church and that his wife had been gloriously saved.

"God uses me in spite of myself," Jake says. "If I had said I was a preacher, that fellow probably would have been turned off. But I'm not a preacher. I'm just a gospel singer."

And for that he is remembered.

O'Neill Terry drove the bus for the Statesmen and the Imperials. He always had a quirk about railroad tracks. Commercial drivers always stop, open the doors and look both ways.

Nancy Dunne, left, has worked for Jake for many years. She is like a member of the Hess family as is Mickey Vaughn, who treasures one of his old toupees.

Jake incessantly kidded Terry about that. One night, Jake was driving and he thought Terry was asleep.

"When Jake came to a crossing, he opened the doors, got out of the bus and put his ear down on the tracks to see if a train was coming," Terry says.

Many years later, Terry was driving a transport truck out of a loading area near Nashville. He struck up a conversation with a young driver and while they were talking Terry mentioned he used to drive the bus for the Statesmen.

The other driver asked if that was the group Jake Hess sang with. When Terry said it was, the younger man said he had once met the singer. Steve Maddox was the young driver's name. When he was 7 or 8, growing up in Nashville, he and a friend, Ricky Mason, were playing games on the telephone. One was on one extension. One was on the other. They would dial a number and when a person would answer they'd curse and hang up.

The boys called this one number and cussed at the man who answered. All the while, the man talked soft and nice. No matter what they said, he didn't get angry. The three of them talked for nearly 90 minutes.

"Who are you?" one of the kids asked.

"Jake Hess, I have a TV show every morning."

"You don't either. You're not even Jake Hess."

They were still cussing when he gave them his telephone number and invited them to call back. Maybe then they'd believe him. When they called again, he invited them to be on TV with him. He asked if one of their mothers was home. He talked to Ricky Mason's mother and told her that if she would have them at a nearby Krystal restaurant by 5 o'clock the next morning that they boys would be guests on his daily television show.

His producers thought Jake had gone mad, that he wouldn't really put two unruly boys on a live television show. But he did. Ricky Mason is dead now, killed in a trucking accident. Steve Maddox, now in his late 30s, still remembers the man who wasn't too busy to talk.

"Tell him that we never did make any more calls like that," Maddox says.

In Atlanta, his singing once allowed Jake a chance to renew a friendship in an unlikely place. He was singing with his children, Becky and Chris. They were working with E.J. Daniel, an evangelist who conducted a prison ministry. That took them behind the massive gates of the Atlanta Federal Penitentiary.

Daniel gave Jake a stack of tracts and asked him to hand them out in the prison yard. There Jake met Big Mo, an inmate who seemed as large as the prison walls that surrounded them.

"What you got in your hands?" Mo grunted.

"Religious tracts."

"What are you going to do with them?"

"I'm supposed to give them out."

With Mo as his escort, Jake soon had given out his literature. Along the way, he invited fellows to come to the singing that evening. At the singing, Jake was reunited with Calvin Newton.

Years before, Newton was a boy tenor in Florida. They sang together in The Melody Masters when the group first moved to South Carolina. By then, he was in prison and most of his gospel music friends had turned away from him. When he told the other prisoners he knew Jake Hess and that he was coming there to sing, nobody believed him. Jake not only came, he brought his children. He introduced them to his old friend, which Newton still remembers.

"Most people in gospel music wouldn't admit they had ever known me, and Jake brought Becky and Chris to see me," Newton says.

When he was released, Newton wanted to sing but no one would let him on a stage, except Jake. He encouraged Newton to reactivate the Sons of Song and he put the quartet on the bus with the Imperials, until another group balked.

"I didn't want to make trouble for Jake so I left," Newton says.

Newton has performed on the Gaither video series several times in recent years. It has been a long way back to gospel music for him. Some of his peers still snub him. But twice Jake has gone to Trenton, Georgia to sing at Newton's church. Chris Hess joined his father for that first visit and Jake didn't know what was coming when Chris suggested they do some quartet songs. Chris invited Buddy Burton out of the audience to sing bass and he wanted Newton—the man he first met in prison—to sing tenor.

Sandy Meador was a jealous little girl in Mississippi when Jake daughter's Becky was born. Sandy thought Jake wouldn't love her anymore after he had his own little girl. Now, decades later, she remains one of his dearest friends and biggest fans.

Younger colleagues also see this side of Jake. Tim Lovelace of the Kingsmen says Jake was his childhood hero. Now he's a friend.

"We were doing a Gaither video and it was lunchtime. The tables were set up in rows, kind of close together. I saw Jake way down at the other end, working his way back and I wondered where he was going. Between us were the cornerstones of gospel music. He was still coming and I got worried his food was getting cold. You know where he was going? To me. He said he just had to stop and say hello," says Lovelace, who made his mark as the self-proclaimed goofy banjo player with the Florida Boys.

Jerry Crutchfield talks about Jake's professional side. A major Nashville producer, he wrote the liner notes for one of Jake's Grammy-winning albums. On Jake's CD with Bradshaw, Crutchfield was the composer of one of the songs. His old friend calls Jake an artist—one of the greatest entertainers of this era.

"When he is introduced and that red light goes on, he is an entertainer. A lot of people make good records. Not many possess the magic of a performer. He exudes this special thing. He is an entertainer, and I know in the confines of gospel music some people may not like that term. But Jake has it all," Crutchfield says.

To Glen Payne of the Cathedrals, Jake is his best friend.

"You have to be called to sing," Payne says. "The Lord has to call you. Some people have a local call instead of a long distance call. Jake was called, and I'm proud to say he's a real good buddy."

The Reverend Michael Guido is one of Jake's oldest friends. The Metter, Georgia evangelist says Jake sings from the heart. "The music and the sermon are not separate. When you sing from the heart there is no division and Jake always sings from the heart. When he sings, anyone could give the invitation for he touches the people."

Young singers such as Ernie Haase of the Cathedrals and McCray Dove of the Dixie Melody Boys have seen first hand what other generations told them about Jake.

"I had one day's rehearsal with The Cathedrals, then we walked out on the stage for the first time together. There, on the front row, was Jake Hess," Haase says. "Afterward, Jake came up to Glen and said he had the number of a great tenor. Then he tore up the number and said, 'Glen, you don't need it. You have the right one.' I will never forget that."

Dove talks about studying Jake's style and about his feeling. "He is *THE* lead singer and it's in the feeling. Anything he sings, you feel what he feels."

Mickey Vaughn and Sandy Meador are both friend and fan to Jake. They have seen him from the audience. They have been there when he was too sick to sing.

"I'm still in awe of him," says Vaughn, a real estate agent in Dallas, Texas. "One night we were talking on the phone and I told him I didn't want him to talk—just listen. I told him he had no idea what he had meant to people. He had never sat on the third or fourth row and felt what people feel when he sings. He can't understand it. He's always been behind the microphone."

For Meador, the little girl who used to stand on the record crates when the Statesmen used to sing in North Mississippi, he represents happiness. "He doesn't realize how many hours, how many days of happiness he's given people. It's not that he performs miracles. It's the joy he brings. The laughing. The smiles he has put in people's lives. He can't relate to that, but it's true. I think about my mother and all my aunts in Mississippi. When you said Jake, they smiled," she says.

Mark Lowry likes to say that Guy Penrod, left, operates a hair farm for Jake and at times Jake himself jokes that The Gaither Vocal Band is his backup group. But in serious moments, Hess says Penrod is the greatest voice to ever come into gospel music.

Lily Fern Weatherford says Jake is a peer who treated her like a peer when she was one of the few women traveling with a quartet on the road. "He made me feel like I was somebody. He made me feel important. The Statesmen, especially Jake, made us feel like we were the most important people at that concert."

Bob Cain thinks of Jake as a gospel singer who was never judgmental of a saloon singer who longed for a new life. Jake even did a duet with the former Birmingham nightclub owner on his first gospel album—just because he asked.

"He never tried to admonish me for my way of life. He just turned me toward a better one. He does it by being Jake, and by the way he lives. You see the faith. I've known him through his sicknesses and he doesn't seem afraid of any-thing. If he had been real judgmental and had come in with fire and brimstone, I don't think we would have become the friends we became," says Cain, who frequently joins Jake and Ivan Parker concerts.

J.D. Sumner remains one of Jake's closest friends. Whenever they're together, old stories come as easily as old songs. To Sumner, Jake is a pioneer.

"Jake has taken gospel music from the dirt road, paved it, and now has a four-lane highway," Sumner says. "The rest of the lead singers who try to achieve the greatness of Jake Hess, when they get to the end of the road, Jake will be standing there waiting on them."

Not that Jake Hess is standing still these days. As Henry Slaughter's lyrics say, God has taken real good care of Jake Hess. He lives on a golf course that's good to him, even though he claims not to keep score anymore. He worships at a church where he's a member, not just a singer. He's with Joyce, and they have been a team nearly 50 years.

When so many of his friends came to celebrate Jake Hess Day in Columbus, Gloria Gaither was among them. On the stage that night, she talked about Jake's achievements. Not about his awards and rewards, but about his children who were there that night, joined by his flock of grand-children.

"So many men who have won gained so many achievements and lost their kids," Gloria Gaither said. "His family is his greatest tribute. They love God and they love each other."

Chris Hess, the minister of youth at the family's home church, often has the opportunity to sing with his father. When they do, he'll joke about Jake's store-bought hair. He's serious about his father, however.

"As long as he can sing, he won't retire. And as long as he's singing he's not retired. He will never retire because it is not a career, this is who he is. Dad's singing is powerful now.

On his old records, he could sing higher and stronger, could jump through more hoops and jump on more pianos. But it wasn't any more powerful. God is still using him in a very real way," Chris Hess says.

Becky Hess Buck long ago retired as a gospel music singer. But not long ago, she joined her father at church to do the recitation on "Sunday Meetin' Time," a song Mosie Lister wrote just for Jake. Big Chief did the original spoken part. Gloria Gaither did it on the *"Jus' Jake"* album. Becky wrote her own words about growing up in a Christian home and what Sunday morning meant to her.

"Now people at Wynnbrook don't even remember me. They say do that song where Becky talks," Jake laughs.

His daughter is thankful for the fruits her father is now harvesting.

"Because the Lord has let this happen, the fruits of all Daddy has done are coming back to him. There has been an outpouring of love. The Lord has let this happen," she says.

Among the fruits, Jake Hess is now enjoying is one that isn't measured by how many CDs are sold or how many people applaud. This blessing came because he was going back on the road to sing and his family wanted someone there to be sure he took his medicine and got his rest. Charged with that mission was Jake Jr., better known as Snake, a smiling young man of nearly 6-foot-4 who has made a career of staying away from gospel music stages.

When Jake arrived in Nashville for a taping of the Statler Brothers TV show with only a baseball cap on his head, Joyce overnighted his hairpiece. To keep things like that from happening again, Snake was hired. Chose whatever title you want for what Snake did but it came down to friend. Years ago, Snake traveled with the Masters V, driving the bus and helping the quartet out in any number of ways. This time, it was much more personal.

"There were sides to Jake I didn't really know. I've come to find out old Snake loves people, loves music and loves the Lord. I've always known he was a good boy, but I didn't know he was so spiritually deep. He's also interested in music. Jake could have been the best singer in the family—including me. He just doesn't care to perform," his father says.

That night in Columbus, when the rest of the family came to the Civic Center stage, one of Jake's children was missing.

"Where's Snake?" Bill Gaither asked.

"Wherever Judy Martin is," the elder Jake joked.

Judy is one-third of the Martins, a popular gospel trio. Jake Jr. and Judy Martin met on the road. She and her sister and brother, like Jake Hess, were often part of the Bill Gaither tour. On November 30, 1996, she also became part of the Hess family. Although Jake Jr. had always avoided the spotlight, they were given a wedding shower at the 1996 Quartet Convention in Louisville, Kentucky.

Jake Jr. stayed out of the spotlight in Columbus that night, but a surprise guest from Atlanta did not. Out of the wings came Hovie Lister, delivering a message from Georgia Governor Zell Miller, his Monday-through-Friday boss. The two old Quartet Men hugged, then, reading from a framed proclamation from the governor, Lister could not be entirely serious.

"I asked the governor why he wasn't giving me one of these. He said because I'm not old enough," Lister laughed. Mostly, he was serious as he looked back on the years he and Jake have spent together.

"God has given Jake what must be his 25th wind," he said. "It's absolute proof that God can do anything."

Jake Hess won't argue with that. He credits God and Bill Gaither—in that order—for all that is happening in his

A few years ago at a National Quartet Convention, Jake Hess Jr. made it a point to go into the main hall to hear a family singing group known as The Martins. The next year, he drove his father to a country church in Butler, Georgia to hear the trio. He liked their music, but more than that, he came to love Judy Martin. In November of 1996, they were married and a few months before people at the Quartet Convention threw them a surprise wedding shower.

career and in his life. He knows he'll always be a Statesmen, but now he has another identity.

Part of his daily routine when he's in Columbus is a morning walk at Peachtree Mall. Wearing a loud, striped shirt, he was walking one morning when a woman stopped him and asked if he was one of the Gaithers, which he admitted.

"I thought so," she said. "I recognized the shirt from one of the videos."

Away from home, he's also part of Gaither's video family. That happened at the 1996 Praise Gathering in Indianapolis. Jake was up early for breakfast when a man at a neighboring table struck up a conversation.

"You here for the Praise Gathering?" he asked.

Jake said he was.

"That Sue Dodge is one great singer, isn't she?"

"She sure is," Jake said.

"Mark Lowry, he's not only funny, he can sing."

Mid-sentence, the man paused.

"Wait a minute," he said to Jake. "I know you. You're Bill Gaither's friend."

Not all of Jake's friends make music. Many of them are people who fill doctors' prescriptions, install air conditioners, pump gas or remember the days they spent in law enforcement. A number of them share a pew with Jake at Wynnbrook Baptist Church.

Hundreds of his friends who know him personally and through his music came to Wynnbrook near the end of 1996. It was two months after the record crowd at the Columbus Civic Center. This Sunday night was supposed to be more intimate. In the end, however, the parking lot was filled and ushers had to bring in metal folding chairs for people who were standing all over the auditorium.

Bill Gaither is family, so when he came to Becky and Brent Buck's home in Georgia, it was natural that he join the Hess family in the kitchen.

Ivan Parker was there along with Bob Cain. Greg Kennard had permission from his pastor at North Highland Assembly of God to be a Baptist that Sunday night. The stage was filled with singers.

"Chris says this is a poor man's Gaither homecoming," Cindy Hess said.

It was a night for friends. Parker told the crowd what it felt like to be on the stage with Jake—"My hero of all heroes." Then, as he sang "Wait 'Til You See Me in My New Home," he did Jake. The hands. The eyes. The pointing fingers. Before the song was over, Jake was doing Jake.

Cain gave his personal testimony, telling how God had radically changed his life. "Life was good," he said. "Or was it?" He remembered when he recorded his first gospel album and how he couldn't wait for Jake to hear it.

"We're having church," Chris Hess said.

It was church, all right, all kinds of church. Kennard played chords on the piano that weren't Baptist chords. Cain played his trumpet, one of those sinful horns that got Jake into trouble so many years before.

A sweet spirit hovered over Wynnbrook that night. Music only set the table. The main course was a simple message first presented 2,000 years ago. It was the gospel, the good news.

That Sunday night, Jake Hess was truly at home.

Joyce sat second row center with Little Brent asleep in her lap.

Jake Jr. was in the vestibule smiling and selling tapes and CDs.

Chris and Becky were sharing the stage with their father.

Cindy Hess, Jake's daughter-in-law, sang the invitation hymn, a peaceful melody that invited people to come just as they are. While eyes were closed and heads bowed, people did come to kneel with pastor Brad Hicks.

When Jake sang "There's Something About That Name," a song written by his friends Bill and Gloria, his grand-daughter, Emmy Shea, did the recitation flawlessly.

"Kings and Kingdoms will all pass away,
but there's something about that name."
They ended the song with a hug.

For Jake Hess, these have become the good old days.

"I don't know how I got here," he says. "I don't know how long I'm staying. I just thank God for the trip."

Acknowledgments

Life is never as simple as it seems and neither is a book that tries to translate a life into words. When we look at a person, we see them from the outside, never knowing the people, places and things that brought them to that day. It is the same with a book. We see only the names on the cover and cannot know all of the people who helped bring to life that subject.

This book is no exception.

Many deserve thanks.

Many deserve credit

Foremost is Jake Hess' family—wife Joyce, daughter

Becky , sons Chris and Jake Jr., son-in-law Brent Buck, daughter-in-laws Cindy and Judy, grandchildren Emmy Shea, Brent , Casey Jake, Natalie, Megan, Lauren and Ansley.

Nancy Dunne provided private phone numbers. Terry Hurley provided scrambled dogs. Friends such as Jerry Crutchfield, Bob Whitaker, Michael Guido, Bill Hancock, Bill Faulkner, Bud Prager, Brad Hicks, Ed Stone, Kaffie Sledge, Don Coker, Buddy Helton, Bill Jarnigan, O'Neill Terry and Charlie Waller provided support.

Jerry Kirksey, Deana Surles and Dennis Zimmerman offered individual assistance as well as help from The Singing News. Tammy Wynette, Larry Gatlin, Rudy Gatlin, Steve Gatlin, Buck White, Bill Anderson and Scotty Moore remind everyone that country music also loves gospel.

Don Cussec of Belmont University, Charles Wolfe of Middle Tennessee State University, Bill Farris and Charles Reagan Wilson of the University of Mississippi, Wayne Flynt of Auburn University; David Evans of the University of Memphis and Bill Malone of Tulane University examined quartet music under an academic microscope.

Gospel singers owe so much to the people who faithfully listen to the music.Three of them, the late Mary B. Jarvis, Mickey Vaughn and Sandy Meador, symbolize those who through the years have filled the seats and bought the records.Their help was invaluable.

The caring support of Bill and Gloria Gaither and all of the talented people who work alongside them in Indiana will never be forgotten.

Finally, there are the quartet people. Although this is the story of one who sang, it is also the story of everyone who has ever stepped on a stage. Those who live and those who have passed away.

These people sat down and talked: J.D. Sumner, Hovie Lister, James Blackwood, Vestal Goodman, Eva Mae LeFevre, Ed Enoch, Ed Hill, George Younce, Glenn Payne, Ernie Haase, Derrell Stewart, Tim Lovelace, Tim Riley, Mark Trammell, David Hill, Bob Crews, Wally Varner, Jim Wesson, McCray Dove, Jack Toney, Dottie Rambo, Calvin Newton, Michael English, Mark Lowry, Buddy Mullins, Mosie and Wylene Lister, Lily Fern Weatherford, Anthony Burger, Larry Ford, Ben Speer, Jim Hill, Jim Hamill, Eldridge Fox, Sherrill Nielsen, Henry Slaughter, Gary McSpadden, Buddy Burton, Rex Nelon, Ace Richman, Don Butler, Gordon Stoker, Ivan Parker, Charles Johnson, Bob Cain, Jack Pittman, Rosa Nell Powell, Mary Tom Reid, John Hall and Cynthia Clawson.